Michel Ezran, Maurizio Morisio
and Colin Tully

Practical Software Reuse

Springer

Michel Ezran
Chief Knowledge Officer, Valtech, Paris, France

Maurizio Morisio, MS, PhD
Research Assistant, Politecnico di Torino, Italy

Colin Tully, MA, Eur Ing, CEng, FBCS
Professor of Software Practice, School of Computing Science, Middlesex University, London, UK

British Library Cataloguing in Publication Data
A catalog record for this book is available from the British Library

Library of Congress Cataloging-in-Publication Data
Ezran, Michel,1967-
     Practical software reuse / Michel Ezran, Maurizio Morisio and Colin Tully.
       p. cm.– (Practitioner series)
     Includes bibliographical references and index.
     ISBN 1-85233-502-5 (alk. paper)
      1. Computer software–Reusability. I. Morisio, Maurizio, 1960- II. Tully, C. J.
     (Colin J.) III. Title. IV. Practitioner series (Springer-Verlag)
     QA76.76.R47 E97 2001
     005–dc21   2001032820

Practitioner series ISSN 1439–9245
ISBN 1–85233–502–5 Springer-Verlag London Berlin Heidelberg
a member of BertelsmannSpringer Science+Business Media GmbH
http://www.springer.co.uk

Typeset by Florence Production, Stoodleigh, Devon, England
Printed and bound by the Athenæum Press Ltd., Gateshead, Tyne & Wear
34/3830–543210 Printed on acid-free paper SPIN 10836924

Series Editor's Foreword

Software reuse, program correctness, user requirements, these are some of the Holy Grails of software and information systems development. If these could be achieved, . . . If only! Software reuse is quite simply expressed by the authors of this excellent exposition on the subject, as

> ". . . the systematic practice of developing software from a stock of building blocks, so that similarities in requirements and/or architecture between applications can be exploited to achieve substantial benefits in productivity, quality and business performance."

It sounds quite straightforward – and for some applications, it is. When my students are given a programming exercise, some surf the Web to find the appropriate code. Without due referencing we call this plagiarism, otherwise it is software reuse! But for large applications, deciding a building block worthy of putting into stock for future use has proved persistently elusive. It suffers from what I have whimsically called

Paul's Law of the IT Concept Fallacy
There exists a belief in IT that any concept can be realised if only enough time and money is spent on the attempt. Such a belief is guaranteed to lead to the spending of much time and money.

My approach to Information Systems is to consider them as models of the organisation, at some level of approximation and of detail. To make the model provide future software reuse, sub-models of the organization would have to be determined, made relatively self-contained, represent a recognizable part of the organization, and be likely to be required as part of some future unknown system. Quite a tall order.

The authors have produced what will become, I suspect, a classic on the subject. The book places a firm emphasis on the practice of reuse, the practical issues affecting success, and a concise review of the important aspects that must be handled concerning reuse. The book is heavily practice based ("evidence-based" practice in the latest fashion), with four in-depth case studies, supplemented by many more short anonymous expositions, and a large number of experience notes relating to the wide practical experiences of the authors.

Whether one ignores the book now, or parts of it, I anticipate that most practitioners involved in software reuse will need to access many parts of this book sooner or later. It is too relevant and valuable to be ignored. So read it now, ready to reuse the knowledge thereby gained.

Ray Paul

Preface

What You Should Know Before Reading This Book

This book seeks throughout to emphasise the *practice* of reuse, and the *practical* issues that influence success or failure. It also seeks to offer a concise coverage of all the important aspects of reuse, focusing on the *essentials* of the subject rather than going into undue depth or detail on some topics at the expense of others.

Why is there a need for such a book? There are four linked reasons. First, effective reuse is of high potential value to most organizations that develop software. Second, reuse can be a difficult and complex subject. Third, awareness and understanding of the potential of reuse, and of how to realise that potential, is absent in a large majority of the organizations that would benefit from it. Fourth, the existing literature lacks a readable and balanced introduction to the practical essentials of reuse.

This guide is dedicated to those who are wondering whether they should adopt reuse and how, and also to those who have already started to adopt it but are wondering where they may be going wrong and how they could do better. It will be of value to business executives, software managers and software developers, whatever kind of software or applications are developed by their organizations, and whatever size those organizations may be.

The book has been produced in the belief that, while reuse can indeed offer highly significant value to most businesses that develop software, nevertheless attempts to adopt reuse, if not based on a sound understanding of all the issues involved, can lead to expensive failure. The authors' purpose, in other words, is to encourage greater understanding of reuse, and in turn to encourage much greater take-up of reuse practices that can transform organizations' software development capability.

The book is founded on two main information sources. The first is the published literature (books, papers in learned journals, conference papers, etc.). This is substantial, and generally excellent, but tends to address specific issues, often in considerable detail, depth and length. It often lacks a solid basis in concrete experience. The risk is that, undiluted, it would mystify, overwhelm or discourage newcomers to the field. We have sought to preserve the essential wisdom offered in the literature, while extracting the practical essentials.

The second source of information is the real-world experience of a number of organizations that have experimented with introducing reuse into their software development practice. This experience base is a distinctive feature of the book, and comprises an important part of its value to readers. Most of the points made in the book are illustrated by means of *experience notes*, drawn from that repository of practical experience.

Acknowledgements

Special thanks are due to a number of people who helped in various ways in the development of this book

Davide Brugali (Politecnico di Torino, Italy) made a major contribution to the preparation of Chapter 7.

Shari Lawrence Pfleeger (System/Software Inc, Washington, DC, USA, and University of Maryland at College Park, MD, USA) and **Sergio Bandinelli** (European Software Institute, Bilbao, Spain) willingly gave their time as reviewers. Their detailed comments were invaluable. They should not be held responsible, however, for defects in the final product, which are to be attributed entirely to the authors.

Of the 19 companies that participated in the survey on which the book is based, four agreed to waive confidentiality agreements so as to allow their experiences to be attributed to them and to be reported in detail (Chapters 8 and 9, and many of the *experience notes* throughout other Chapters of the book). The utmost gratitude is due to these companies, and to their representatives, whose additional collaboration was invaluable in contributing to the special character of the book. They are: **Pascal Maheut** (Thomson-CSF Technologies et Méthodes, France); **Angela Lo Surdo**, **Elisabetta Morandin** and **Cristina Lisoni** (Sodalia, Italy); **Manuel Villalba** (Eliop SA, Spain); and **Colin Woodgate** (Chase Computer Services, UK).

The survey work was undertaken as part of a project (project number 23960: SURPRISE), funded by the **European Commission** within a programme entitled ESSI (European Systems and Software Initiative). The 24 projects surveyed were themselves also funded as part of the same programme. The main deliverable from SURPRISE was a first version of this book, privately produced for restricted distribution to selected European organizations. This first public edition contains major updates and revisions to the original restricted-circulation version.

Contents

Readers' Guide

Chapter Outlines – the Book at a Glance

The following is a chapter-by-chapter summary of what the book contains.

Chapter 1: Introducing Software Reuse
This opening chapter offers an overview of the main issues in software reuse. It defines what we mean by reuse, and discusses a number of fundamental concepts essential to a balanced understanding of reuse.

Chapter 2: Reusable Software Assets
The concept of reusable assets is central to software reuse. If we consider reuse as a way of capturing and exploiting business expertise, the word 'asset' is seen to be very appropriate. Software assets encapsulate business knowledge and are of high value for a company. This chapter defines what assets are, explains what makes them reusable and describes their life-cycle.

Chapter 3: Reuse Repository
The repository is the place where reusable software assets are stored, along with the catalogue of assets. Everybody should be aware that it contains important company know-how, and should be able to access and use it easily. In this chapter we take the point of view of a technical manager charged with setting up the reuse repository for her company. First, we describe the repository in terms of the functions it should offer. We then examine some families of tools on the market that offer these functions.

Chapter 4: Reuse Processes
How should reuse be practised, introduced and improved? The aim of this chapter is to present reuse processes, and to understand why they are necessary, how they relate to traditional software processes, and how they are defined and implemented in the field.

Chapter 5: Managing Reuse
This chapter discusses three management requirements that are of critical importance to the success of a reuse initiative, and which concern both business managers and software managers. They are: to decide whether the organization should embark on a systematic reuse initiative; to gain maximum commitment to, and involvement in, the reuse initiative; and to decide on the allocation of reuse-specific responsibilities.

Chapter 6: Reuse Metrics

What to measure and how? After having pointed out important issues to be measured, this chapter proposes a measurement approach based on business goals (applying the GQM framework).

Chapter 7: Reuse Techniques and Technologies

Several techniques have been proposed to maximize the reuse of components, of architectural designs, and even of designers' experience in solving domain-specific problems. These techniques are partial in their life-cycle coverage and in the viewpoints that they represent. This chapter reviews the contributions and usefulness of some of these techniques.

Chapter 8: Two Major Case Histories

This chapter presents a description of two of the most significant reuse experiences in Europe. Sodalia (Italy) and Thomson-CSF (France) appear to be very successful in reuse. There are interesting similarities and differences both in their business context and their approach to reuse. The cases are presented in parallel.

Chapter 9: Two Smaller Case Histories

This chapter presents a description of successful reuse as experienced in two smaller European companies – ELIOP (Spain) and Chase Computer Services (UK). As in the previous chapter the two cases are presented in parallel.

Chapter 10: Experience Review and Success Factors

The reuse experience base created for this book contains data on projects undertaken in 19 companies which have embarked on significant reuse programmes. This concluding chapter provides a synthesis of that collected experience, in terms of recurring patterns and success/failure factors.

Reading Strategies for Those with Limited Time

Of course, we hope you will read the whole book. We have kept it concise to encourage you to do so. As realists, however, we accept that your time is precious, and that your interests may not be evenly distributed across all the topics covered in the book. If you have to sample, the following are some recommendations.

Business managers

Recommended minimum reading is **Chapter 1** (Introducing Software Reuse), **Chapter 5** (Managing Reuse) and **Chapter 10** (Experience Review and Success Factors).

If more time is available, it is well worth looking at **Chapter 4** (Reuse Processes) and **Chapters 8** and **9** (Reuse Histories).

Software managers

After following the recommendations for business managers, go on to read **Chapter 2** (Reusable Software Assets), **Chapter 3** (Reuse Repository) and **Chapter 6** (Reuse Metrics). These cover the three essential areas of reuse practice, which it is important to understand if you are involved in the management of a reuse programme.

Software developers

Developers are recommended not to omit any chapters, even those aimed mainly at managers: remember, it is important for you to know what your managers know! The one remaining chapter, specially for you, is **Chapter 7** (Reuse Techniques and Technologies). Even if you do not regard yourself as a programming whiz-kid, it's worth scanning this chapter to get a starter's guide to recent advances in technical practice.

Author Biographies

Michel Ezran, Valtech, France

Michel Ezran is Chief Knowledge Officer at the Paris office of Valtech, a leading international e-business consulting firm operating in eight countries across Europe, North America and Asia. Valtech provides complete e-business solutions, encompassing strategy, communication and IT, with services including full project delivery, skills transfer and consulting.

As the leader of Valtech's corporate Knowledge Management programme, Michel manages a team of knowledge managers, a worldwide network of experts and Valtech's enterprise portal. He joined Valtech as staff number 10, and has successively held positions of Senior Consultant and R&D Manager. As a consultant, he advised companies in migrating their business information systems to new technologies (Java, CORBA, UML, EJB, internet), including not only the technology aspects but also architecture, process, organisation and management, and helped software organisations to improve their processes through the adoption of reuse and business components.

He has also acted as consultant to advanced technology projects, on the coordination of development teams, on monitoring development phases (requirements capture, object analysis, architecture definition, object design, coding and testing) and on managing the risks arising from migration to new technologies.

Prior to Valtech, he worked for Cap Gemini in France and South America, and for other software houses, with experience on a variety of software development projects in the field of business information systems.

michel.ezran@valtech.fr
http://www.valtech.com

Maurizio Morisio, Politecnico di Torino, Italy

Dr Morisio is a research assistant in the Dipartimento di Automatica e Informatica, Politecnico di Torino, Turin, Italy. He recently spent two years working with the Experimental Software Engineering Group at the

University of Maryland. During that time he was co-director of the Software Engineering Laboratory (SEL), a consortium of NASA Goddard Space Flight Center, the University of Maryland and Computer Science Corporation, which has the mission of improving software practices at NASA and CSC.

The overall goal of Maurizio's research and consulting is to understand how software is produced and maintained, in order to improve software processes and products in industrial settings. Software production involves three main dimensions (processes; people and organisation; tools and technology) and his activity has spanned all three, including work on object-oriented technology (analysis, design and programming), software product lines, framework-based development, COTS-based development, processes and measures for individuals and small teams (PSP, PIPSI) and the evaluation and selection of tools. His current focus is on open source development and service engineering for the wireless internet.

His approach to both research and consulting is strongly empirical: observing and analysing facts rather than trusting claims and hype, and using empirical methods such as case studies, experiments and surveys. He has a PhD in software engineering and a MSc in electronic engineering from Politecnico di Torino.

morisio@polito.it
http://morserv.polito.it/morisio/

Colin Tully, Middlesex University, UK

Colin Tully is Professor of Software Practice in the School of Computing Science at Middlesex University, London, UK. The School is one of the largest computing science departments in Britain, oriented strongly toward the applied end of the discipline. Its strengths lie in areas such as human-computer interaction modelling and design, usability, systems failures, systems and software processes and their improvement, development methods, neural networks, vision and image processing, multimedia programming, hypermedia authoring, digital libraries, mobile and personal technologies, medical informatics, and telematics.

Colin's primary interests are the study of failures in software-based systems, and of methods of improving organisational capability for avoiding such failures. He is currently involved in the establishment of the Centre for Systems Forensics and Capability (CSFC) at Middlesex. Previously he practised for twelve years as an independent consulting software and systems engineer.

He holds an Economics degree from Cambridge University, and has worked continuously in the field of software and systems since graduating in 1960. In his first job, at LEO Computers, he was one of a two-man team who machine-coded the LEO III Master Routine, the world's first commercial multi-programming operating system. He subsequently gained wide experience in systems development, consultancy, education and training, academic and industrial research, and academic and industrial management, including periods at the London School of Economics and the University of York. He was extensively involved in industrial collaborative projects, funded both by the UK government and the European Commission, on software development environments and software process improvement.

He has served as programme chair or committee member for a large number of conferences, is editor-in-chief of the journal *Software Process: Improvement and Practice*, and has many publications to his name. He is a European Engineer, UK Chartered Engineer, and Fellow of the British Computer Society.

c.tully@mdx.ac.uk
http://www.cs.mdx.ac.uk

Introducing Software Reuse   1

ABSTRACT

This opening Chapter offers an overview of the main issues in software reuse. It defines what we mean by reuse, and discusses a number of fundamental concepts essential to a balanced understanding of reuse.

1.1 First of All . . .

Of his many accomplishments, Erwin Schumacher is best remembered for telling us that 'small is beautiful'. His phrase became established in the late twentieth century mindset.

Software reuse, the subject of this book, is about a twofold promise, that software projects can be small, and that they can create beautiful software – that is if you accept that high quality, in the form of clean design, fitness for purpose and a low defect count, constitutes 'beauty' in software.

We have become accustomed to software projects that are ugly and uncontrollable monsters, devouring seemingly endless resources, and delivering products that are ill-structured, over-sized and bug-infested, and which often fail to meet our real needs. Under the name of 'the software crisis' we have accepted that state of things for thirty years. Fred Brooks' familiar and well-argued assertion that there is 'no silver bullet' may paradoxically have made things worse: convince people that there is no one simple medicine, and they may shrink from undergoing more radical treatments.

Properly understood, and deployed in the right context, reuse offers the opportunity to achieve radical improvement. It should still, however, not be regarded as a silver bullet, a simple recipe that we can depend on to rid us of monstrous projects and bad software.

In one sense this is a modest book. It seeks to present just the essentials of software reuse. It is neither an academic textbook, nor a cookbook with ready-made recipes telling practitioners or managers 'how to do it'. It offers, simply and without unnecessary detail or jargon, an introductory overview of the issues involved in the successful practice of reuse.

In another sense, however, the book's aim is far from modest. It is to set out the vision and concepts of reuse, and the experiences of some of its pioneers, in the hope that you may be encouraged to think about adopting reuse yourself as a new way of life. It aims, in other words, to be a gateway to the wonderland of reuse. If it succeeds in meeting that aim for you, so that you pass through the gateway, then will be the time to start exploring the large (and rapidly growing) body of excellent detailed literature on reuse, for more detailed information on cost models, class libraries, organizational structures, repository management, reuse maturity assessments, framework and component technologies and many other important issues. For now, we hope you will find in these pages excitement, surprise, challenge and new visions of what it is possible to achieve in the difficult business of creating software.

1.2 Definition and Basic Essentials

The objective of this introductory Chapter is to present an outline map of the reuse landscape, identifying the essential ideas of software reuse, before they are developed further in later Chapters. We start with a definition.

Definition

> Software reuse is the systematic practice of developing software from a stock of building blocks, so that similarities in requirements and/or architecture between applications can be exploited to achieve substantial benefits in productivity, quality and business performance.

A definition cannot include everything that might be said about the term being defined. It should incorporate a choice of features that are necessary and sufficient for understanding the term. The above definition is based on four key features of software reuse.

- Reuse is a systematic software development practice.

- Reuse employs a stock of building blocks.

- Reuse exploits similarities in requirements and/or architecture between applications.

- Reuse offers substantial benefits in productivity, quality and business performance.

Let's now look at each of those ideas in turn.

1.2.1 Reuse Is a Systematic Software Development Practice

Software reuse has a wide spectrum of possible meanings. On the one hand, it is possible to interpret much of the progress in software practice in the past half-century in terms of increasing levels of reuse (see Section 1.4, later in this Chapter). On the other hand, advanced and sophisticated approaches to reuse exist at the current leading edge between research and practice, which are probably outside the competence range of most software developing organizations (so-called *generative reuse* is an example). The definition does not embrace that whole range of meanings, but focuses attention on the centre of the range – an approach to reuse which is practically feasible for most developers here and now, which is a substantial advance on accepted practice, and which can offer major benefits.

One result of that definition strategy is the inclusion of the word 'systematic'. 'What about non-systematic reuse', you may have wondered; 'isn't that still reuse?' You are right: of course it is! Strictly we have offended against logic in defining reuse as only a part of itself. It's like equating soccer with just the premier league game, or describing drama just in terms of Molière, Pirandello and Shakespeare.

The justification for offending against logic in that way is that it is not possible, except by undertaking software reuse *systematically*, to realize the bold claims made on its behalf. It is the bold claims, the large benefits, and the substantial commitment needed to achieve them, that form the subject-matter of this book. We do not want to waste your time telling you about something that is everyday or casual, but rather to set out a big vision of how software capability can be transformed. Having said that, what distinguishes systematic from non-systematic reuse?

Some of the key features of the systematic practice of software reuse are set out in *Fig. 1.1*. Non-systematic reuse is, by contrast, ad hoc, dependent on individual knowledge and initiative, not deployed consistently throughout the organization, and subject to little if any management planning and control. If the parent software organisation is reasonably mature and well managed, it is not impossible for non-systematic reuse to achieve some good results. The more probable outcome, however, is that non-systematic reuse is chaotic in its effects, feeds the high-risk culture of individual heroics and fire-fighting, and amplifies problems and defects rather than damping them.

SYSTEMATIC SOFTWARE REUSE MEANS . . .

Understanding how reuse can contribute toward the goals of the whole business.

Defining a technical and management strategy to achieve maximum value from reuse.

Integrating reuse into the total software process, and into the software process improvement programme.

Ensuring all software staff have the necessary competence and motivation.

Establishing appropriate organisational, technical and budgetary support.

Using appropriate measurements to control reuse performance.

Fig. 1.1 Systematic software reuse.

1.2.2 Reuse Employs a Stock of Building Blocks

The term 'building block' is used in the definition because the properties of physical building blocks, and the way we use them, are well understood, and they convey very well the conceptual flavour that is appropriate for explaining software reuse. Let us consider some of those properties (*Fig. 1.2*).

Building blocks are not only children's playthings. The concept is widespread throughout industry, and it is intrinsic to product breakdown structures. The design of a subsystem, assembly, sub-assembly or part may be common to several different models of motor car, washing machine, industrial pump or machine tool. Even the complete architecture of a product may be carried over from one model to subsequent models. Reusable building blocks are fundamental to the goal of not reinventing the wheel, and to

Building blocks are artefacts, which can be put together to make larger-scale artefacts.

They may or may not have been designed primarily for use as building blocks (compare a box of toy blocks with off-cut pieces of wood).

They may or may not have been designed to fit together in a standard way (compare a box of toy blocks with the Lego system).

The greater the diversity of building blocks (in terms, for instance, of size, shape, colour, material), the greater the diversity of structures that can be created from them.

If a building block has unusual properties, its use is likely to be restricted to a smaller number of specific structures. The more general its properties, the more general its use.

There may be large building blocks that define a partial 'architecture' into which smaller ones can be fitted (for example, a Lego baseboard or chassis).

Building blocks may be combined into sub-assemblies, so that a sub-assembly can then be incorporated into various different end-products.

Fig. 1.2 Some important properties of building blocks.

making progress by building on previous experience of what works. It has been central to industrial development for the past two centuries.

Software reuse is based on exactly the same concepts as children's building blocks or reusable designs in industry. Although systematic reuse is not yet widely practised in software development, it will be seen in the future to be as essential to progress in software as it has been to progress in manufacturing and other sectors of industry.

In the software reuse literature, building blocks are most commonly called *reusable assets* (or *reuse assets*; often just *assets* for short), and we will use those terms from now on. Assets are work products of any kind, from any part of the software process. 'Asset' is an appropriate word, since software work products capture knowledge that is important to the enterprise, and therefore carry potential value. Reuse is a powerful means of exploiting that value-adding potential.

Assets may be of a technical or management nature, large-grained or fine-grained, simple or composite. They may have varying degrees of *leverage* (leverage is said to occur when reuse of one asset makes possible the reuse of a chain of other related assets further 'downstream' in the process). The belief by some people that source code modules are the only kind of reusable assets is mistaken; assets may include such things as requirements, project plans, estimates, architectures, designs, user interfaces, test plans, test cases, data, quality plans, and documentation. The concept of reusable assets is developed more fully in Chapter 2.

The definition refers to 'a *stock* of building blocks'. If that stock comprises more than a small number of items, we need to make arrangements to know what items we have, where to find them and whether they are worth keeping; otherwise we will not derive the best return from having established the stock. In this respect, a stock of reusable software assets is no different from any other kind of stock. A small shopkeeper can see or remember the contents of his store-room; the big store needs techniques of stock control and management. Managing a stock of reusable software assets, described in Chapter 3, uses concepts such as the asset *catalogue* and the asset *repository*.

Having an effective catalogue is often essential in achieving systematic reuse. Its absence can be a major contributor to chaos. It is rather like the situation, familiar no doubt to many parents, where Lego blocks are scattered all over the house, in every room, so that you don't know which ones you've got, the ones you need you can't find, and the ones you find by chance you probably don't need.

If a catalogue lists what assets we have and where they are stored, then a repository (like a library or a warehouse) is where we store and retrieve them. Reusable software assets may be stored in a single repository, or there may be multiple repositories: that is like the difference between keeping all Lego blocks in a single big box, or keeping the members of different sets in their separate boxes.

As can be easily imagined, how to design repositories for reusable software is of great interest to those of a technical inclination, and there is much discussion of it in the technical literature. Should we use database technology, or a configuration management system, or the repository of an integrated software engineering environment? Should the catalogue and repository functions be combined or separate? How should assets be classified for storage and retrieval, and how should search requirements be specified?

As already indicated, such questions may not be important to small software organisations (like small shopkeepers), whose asset collection is not big or complex enough to justify such a volume of technical fire-power. In this book the intention is to limit the discussion of catalogue and repository questions to the essential issues, and not to become entangled with too many technicalities.

1.2.3 Reuse Exploits Similarities in Requirements and/or Architecture Between Applications

This key idea is discussed in two stages. First, we will discuss what is meant by an application, and some related concepts. Second, we will look at how the potential for reuse arises from fundamental similarities between applications.

What Is Meant by Applications?

For our purposes, an *application* means a collection of one or more programs, together with all necessary supporting work products, that undertake some substantial user function. It may be alternatively called a system or a product in some contexts. Examples of applications might include word processing, payroll, engine control, seat reservations, vehicle routing, survey analysis and so on.

Note that the term *application domain*, which is an important concept in software reuse, is not the same as an individual *application*. The application domain of word processing, for example, refers to the general problem area of word processing. By contrast, an individual word processing application represents one specific solution within that general problem area. The same distinction applies in the case of payroll, engine control, and the other applications listed as examples in the previous paragraph.

An enterprise may develop one or more applications in the same domain. The need for different applications may arise because of the existence of a range of users with different needs, and/or because of changes in user needs over time.

The possibility of employing reuse to handle changes over time raises the question of whether maintenance is a form of reuse. Opinions differ. We would propose that maintenance and reuse are in principle independent, but in practice may be related. Maintenance, like initial development, can (but need not) employ reusable assets; reusable assets, like all software, need to be maintained.

There is no universal or clear-cut way of defining the boundaries between one application and another within a domain, or between one domain and another. Different organizations define such boundaries according to their own perceptions and business circumstances. In some cases organizations refer to applications in a common domain as a *product line*. Software product lines are discussed briefly later in this Chapter.

What Is the Source of Similarities Between Applications?

Why is it that a piece of source code, for example, or any other kind of asset, might prove to be usable in the context of two or more different applications, in the same domain or even perhaps in different domains? The reason must obviously be that there is a demand that the applications have in common, that can be satisfied by using common assets. The applications are *similar* in respect of that common demand.

A good illustration is provided by Reed (1995).[1] 'On Wall Street, some companies are structured as several small development teams, each supporting a trader. Most, if not all, of these teams are building similar applications. This type of development organization can capitalize substantially on software reuse.'

Of course, if two applications were similar in every respect, they would be identical. In that case, there would be no need to design and build the application a second time: the original application would simply be replicated. (Mere replication of a complete application is not regarded as reuse, according to the conventional usage of the term – just as we do not conventionally say that every Fiat Uno car is a *reuse* of the Fiat Uno design.) Thus, reuse of assets between one application and another is dependent on there being *both similarities and differences* between the applications – just as there are similarities and differences between the Uno and other Fiat models. The more similarities exist, the more potential there is for assets to be reused.

There are two ultimate sources of similarities among applications – their *requirements* and their *architecture*. Requirements specify the *problem*, that is the objectives of an application, in terms of a set of characteristics with which the eventual specific solution must comply. An architecture specifies what might be called a general category or mode of *solution*. Both requirements and architecture thus constrain or delimit the solution space within which the specific solution must be located, and it is those constraints or delimitations that are the root causes of similarities and differences between applications.

The process of determining requirements begins at the start of a project, and may continue, at greater or lesser intensity, until close to the end. Early attention focuses on high-level (or whole-system, or user) requirements. Those early requirements lead to design decisions that in turn generate further requirements at lower levels, perhaps for individual subsystems or parts.

Requirements may address any of the dimensions of the solution space, which include functionality, performance, reliability, maintainability, user interface, cost, delivery date, operational platform (hardware and software), development platform (methods, languages and tools), portability, length of life, interactions with other systems (support systems, peer systems and contextual systems) and so on. Adopting a specified architecture may itself, in some circumstances, be a high-level requirement; conversely, it may be a design decision arising from the need to meet other requirements. In either case, adopting a specific architecture is likely to influence downstream requirements. In other words, requirements and architecture may not be wholly independent of each other.

Architectures are commonly thought of as defining categories or modes of solutions in three of the above dimensions: functionality, user interface, and operational platform. *Functional architectures* relate to application domains, and are consequently often referred to as domain architectures. Domain architectures are very important in reuse, and a good deal will be said about them later. *User interface architectures* define stylistic features of interfaces, such as menus, forms, command lines, hot buttons and so on, and the ways in which they are combined. *Operational platform architectures* (often called implementation architectures) define common patterns in which hardware, operating systems, other software utilities and middleware are configured to provide the infrastructural support which the application-specific software uses. User interface and operational platform architectures relate to what may be called technical domains.

In general, the term *vertical reuse* is used to refer to reuse which exploits functional similarities in a single application domain. It is contrasted with *horizontal reuse*, which exploits similarities across two or more application domains. There are two forms of horizontal reuse. The first refers to the exploitation of functional similarities across different domains; an example might be loans and reservations functions in the domains of libraries and car hire. The second refers to the exploitation of similarities in technical domains (user interface and operational platform), which are independent of application domains. This distinction is discussed further in Chapter 2.

Opportunities for reuse are like defects: the sooner they are found the better. If a defect is introduced during requirements definition, and is found at the same stage, the cost of correction is small; if it is not found until, say, a late stage of testing, the cost can be enormous. Likewise, if similarities between applications are identified at the stage when requirements and architecture are being determined, and if that leads at once to a recognition of opportunities for reuse, the potential benefit is hugely greater than if the opportunity is only recognized at, say, the coding stage.

Note that we say 'potential benefit'. Whether the benefit can be fully realized doesn't depend only on early recognition of similarities and of the corresponding reuse opportunities. It also depends on how well the 'flow-down' from requirements and architectural decisions to later downstream decisions was recorded in the earlier system. If it was well recorded, then the chances of 'replaying' that flowdown in the new application are high, which means that a greater number of downstream assets can be reused and high leverage can be achieved.

We are now encountering again the difference between systematic and non-systematic reuse. Non-systematic reuse depends upon individuals casually recognizing similarities at any stage of development, based on their previous experience with other applications. It depends on their using their own initiative about whether to exploit those similarities, and whether to pass the information on to colleagues (who might or might not make use of it). Systematic reuse means a continual conscious and organized search for reuse opportunities in all work products, so that the opportunities are detected as early as possible, and so that maximum leverage is obtained. It also means augmenting the chances that future applications can exploit reuse opportunities, by building in traceability from upstream requirements and architecture decisions to other downstream work products.

Let us try to summarize. Opportunities for reuse from one application to another originate in their having similar requirements, or similar architectures, or both. The search for similarities should begin as close as possible to those points of origin – that is, when requirements are identified and architecture decisions are made. The possibilities for exploiting similarities should be maximized by having a development process that is designed and managed so as to give full visibility to the flowdown from requirements and architecture to all subsequent work products.

1.2.4 Reuse Offers Substantial Benefits in Productivity, Quality and Business Performance

Perhaps you are beginning to think that reuse seems a lot of effort. Right! In that case, you may also be wondering whether it is worth it. That is the question to which we now turn.

In orderly systems, you don't get something for nothing, and big changes usually demand big and sustained efforts. It is only by resting content in the arms of chaos that you open yourself to the chance of a small cause leading to a large change. Unfortunately, in a state of chaos, any change is unpredictable, and its effects are as likely to be harmful as they are to be beneficial. Prominent management writers have some striking things to say about achieving big changes for the better: see *Fig. 1.3*.

What companies require is seldom anything so 'reasonable' and 'realistic' as a 10 per cent improvement in some performance measure or other. What we actually require is more often something like a 50 per cent improvement, or a 75 per cent improvement.
(Michael Hammer/James Champy, talking about business process reengineering)

Good things happen only when planned; bad things happen on their own . . . One doesn't just go from awful to wonderful in a single bound.
(Philip Crosby, talking about quality)

Tackling a difficult problem is often a matter of seeing where the high leverage lies, a change which – with a minimum of effort – would lead to lasting significant improvement. High-leverage changes are usually non-obvious. So people shift the burden of the problem to other solutions – well intentioned, easy fixes, which seem extremely efficient. Unfortunately the easier solutions only treat the symptoms; they leave the underlying problem unaltered . . . and the system loses whatever abilities it had to solve the underlying problem.
(Peter Senge, talking about learning organizations)

Fig. 1.3 Some views on business change.

What these writers agree in saying, in different ways and from different viewpoints, is (a) big changes are both necessary and possible, (b) the changes we undertake should address business-critical problems and be based on understanding the root causes of those problems, (c) the changes will take a lot of sustained effort, but (d) the resulting value can far outweigh the effort. Experience shows that those propositions are all relevant to software reuse.

Reuse may generate value from three kinds of improvement: productivity, quality and business performance.

Productivity improvements arise essentially because reuse means less effort through writing less (there are two ways to increase productivity: write faster, or write less, and writing less is easier!). Higher productivity through reduced effort leads in turn to lower development costs and shorter time to market. It can also lead to higher quality (see the next paragraph).

Quality improvements arise in two ways. First, if assets have achieved proven quality in one project, that quality can be carried over to another. Second, if the effort on a project is substantially reduced, there will be fewer defects. Higher quality in turn leads to lower maintenance and service costs, and higher customer satisfaction.

Beware, however! The quality argument has hidden risks. Reusers must not take the original quality of reused assets for granted, nor assume that what constitutes quality in one context necessarily constitutes quality in a different context. Further, substantial reductions in effort may lure reusers into assuming that the development task is easier than it really is, and may induce carelessness.

Business performance improvements of course include lower costs, shorter time to market, and higher customer satisfaction, which have already been noted under the headings of productivity and quality improvements. They also include improved predictability (smaller amounts of effort are more predictable than larger ones). Such benefits can in turn initiate a virtuous circle of higher profitability, growth, greater competitiveness, increased market share, entry to new markets and so on. These benefits may be direct, if the company's main business is software, or indirect if the software it develops is embedded in its products or supports its business processes.

Let us now look at some examples of estimated benefits that have been reported from systematic software reuse: see *Fig. 1.4.* The examples cover the use of various programming languages, ranging from Ada to Cobol and C++. The examples are presented in alphabetical order of company.

These estimates should be treated with a degree of caution. They all claim improvements in a *key performance indicator*, such as productivity, quality or cycle time; in some cases those improvements are set against a *level of reuse* (which roughly means the proportion of the total work product that was reused). We do not know how those measures were calculated or the reliability of the values obtained. They should therefore be treated as being subject to perhaps substantial margins of error, and as presenting rather rough impressions of achievement. We should not, however, throw out the baby with the bathwater: however error-prone or ill-defined, these impressions are impressive.

The examples compare a situation with reuse against a situation without reuse. The comparison may be done in one of two ways. The first way is to compare the *actual* values of a performance indicator at two points in time, one before the introduction of reuse and one after; note that the length of the time lapse is in no case stated. The second way is to compare the *estimated* value of a performance indicator for a project without reuse against the *actual* value with reuse.

The examples are of claimed results in practice. An alternative way of investigating the potential of reuse is shown in Table 1.1, which sets out a range of *hypothetical* possibilities for the purposes of illustration. It assumes the ability to estimate a *reduction factor* and a *reuse index*. The reduction factor (column 1) is an indicator of what is saved on average (in terms, say, of effort, time or cost) for those work products that exploit reuse. The reuse index (column 2) is an indicator of the proportion of the total work product that exploits reuse: it is closely related to the concept of reuse level as shown in

- DEC
  - *cycle time*: 67%–80% lower (reuse levels 50%–80%)

- First National Bank of Chicago
  - *cycle time*: 67%–80% lower (reuse levels 50%–80%)

- Fujitsu
  - *proportion of projects on schedule*: increased from 20% to 70%
  - *effort to customize package*: reduced from 30 person-months to 4 person-days

- GTE
  - *cost*: $14M lower (reuse level 14%; baseline costs not specified)

- Hewlett-Packard
  - *defects*: 24% and 76% lower (two projects)
  - *productivity*: 40% and 57% higher (same two projects)
  - *time to market*: 42% lower (one of the above two projects)

- NEC (Nippon Electric Company)
  - *productivity*: 6.7 times higher
  - *quality*: 2.8 times better

- Raytheon
  - *productivity*: 50% higher (reuse level 60%)

- Toshiba
  - *defects*: 20%–30% lower (reuse level 60%)

- Sample of 75 projects in 15 companies
  - *quality*: 10 times better (reuse levels 10%–18%)

- Sample of 15 projects in 9 companies (reuse levels up to about 95%)
  - *productivity*: 10 times higher than cross-industry benchmark
  - *time to market*: 70% lower than cross-industry benchmark
  - *cost*: 84% lower than cross-industry benchmark

Fig. 1.4 Some reported estimates of actual improvements due to reuse.

Fig 1.4. Multiplying the reduction factor and the reuse index gives an indicator of the broad level of *overall savings* (column 3) that can in principle be achieved, ranging from one-quarter of total development effort, time or cost to nearly three-quarters.

The important thing to realize about this table is that the values shown for both the reduction factors (50 per cent to 80 per cent) and the reuse index (50 per cent to 90 per cent) are known to be achievable in practice. Although it is hypothetical, therefore, it is nevertheless realistic.

It is worth spending some time reflecting carefully on the reported and hypothetical figures presented in Fig. 1.4 and Table 1.1, and asking what the effect

Table 1.1 *Illustrations of hypothetical levels of savings.*

Reduction factor (reduction in effort, time or cost achieved for work products that are developed with reuse) [1]	Reuse index (proportion of total effort, time or cost attributable to work products that are developed with reuse) [2]	Overall savings (saving in total development effort, time or cost achieved as a result of reuse) [3] = [1] × [2]
50%	50%	25%
50%	70%	35%
50%	90%	45%
60%	50%	30%
60%	70%	42%
60%	90%	54%
70%	50%	35%
70%	70%	49%
70%	90%	63%
80%	50%	40%
80%	70%	56%
80%	90%	72%

would be if you could achieve comparable results in your business. Then you will be ready to ask the next question – whether you are prepared to undertake the substantial, sustained and systematic effort without which such results are not achievable.

1.3 Some Further Introductory Essentials

With the four main ideas about software reuse now in place, we will look in this Section at some other related ideas that are important for completing the outline map of the reuse landscape which Chapter 1 aims to present. They are as follows.

● There are various routes by which assets achieve reuse.

● There is an important relationship between reuse and software process maturity.

● Reuse is an investment, whether or not you call it that.

● Reuse may be pursued within the wider business context of product line practice.

1.3.1 There Are Various Routes by Which Assets Achieve Reuse

This is a surprisingly complicated matter, which we will try to present as simply as possible. The route to reuse is determined by the answers to seven questions, as set out in *Fig. 1.5*.

The answers to those seven questions are in principle independent – meaning there are 288 different routes for an asset to be reused! Some of the combinations, however, are less probable than others. Some comments on the above questions and answers may be helpful.

1 What was the original source of the asset?
 - It was developed in-house.
 - It was acquired externally.

2 What was the original purpose of the asset (with respect to reuse)?
 - It was intended for immediate use on a specific project, without reuse in mind.
 - It was intended for immediate use on a specific project, with reuse in mind.
 - It was intended not for immediate use on a specific project, but entirely for purposes of reuse.

3 Was the asset reengineered for reuse (prior to its current reuse)?
 - It was reengineered for reuse at some earlier time (eg to be put into a reuse repository).
 - It has remained unchanged since its original development or acquisition.

4 Was the asset designed for reuse by setting parameters (grey box reuse)?
 - It has grey box capability.
 - It does not have grey box capability.

5 Was the asset retrieved from a repository for its current reuse?
 - It was retrieved from a repository.
 - It was in a repository but not retrieved from it.
 - It was not in a repository.

6 Was it necessary to 'look inside' the asset in order to assess whether it meets the requirements for reuse (glass box reuse)?
 - Glass box reuse was necessary.
 - Glass box reuse was not necessary.

7 Was it necessary to reengineer the asset for its current reuse (white box reuse)?
 - White box reuse was necessary.
 - White box reuse was not necessary.

NOTE: the terms 'glass box', 'grey box' and 'white box' reuse are explained below.

Fig. 1.5 Some of the factors influencing the life history of a reusable asset.

Some people say that buying an asset (question 1) is itself a form of reuse. Their reason is presumably that selling the asset to many customers means it is being reused. That, however, is true only in the trivial sense that selling many cars of the same design represents reuse. It does not, in itself, constitute systematic reuse as defined in this book. Of course, the vendor of the asset may have employed systematic reuse in developing it; and the buyer of the asset may employ it as a reusable asset in a systematic reuse programme. In principle, however, acquisition and reuse are independent concepts, just as we have argued that maintenance and reuse are independent.

A reusable asset may exist in many versions throughout its lifecycle, including being reengineered specifically to make it (more) reusable (questions 3 and 7). This indicates the important need for configuration management in reuse, and for the careful control of maintenance on reusable assets. Reengineering is one of two ways in which an asset may be adapted for reuse; the other is by setting parameters (question 4). Adaptation by setting parameters is only possible if the asset has been designed that way, either originally or by subsequent reengineering. Setting parameters means making selections among predesigned sets of options, so as to determine the exact properties of the asset.

If an asset is reused without the need for any adaptation, that is known as *black box reuse*. If reengineering is necessary, that is to say if it is necessary to change the internal body of an asset in order to obtain the required properties, that is known as *white box reuse*. The intermediate situation, where adaptation is achieved by setting parameters, is known as *grey box reuse*. *Glass box reuse* refers to the situation where it is necessary to 'look inside' an asset, on a 'read-only' basis, in order to discover its properties, in the case where the available description of those properties is inadequate.

A final note concerns the continuing usefulness, or value, of reusable assets. In just the same way that the fitness of software in general is known to decay as a result of increasing age and continuing maintenance, so the fitness of a reusable software asset decays with age and maintenance. The reasons for this are well understood, and derive from the difficulty of maintaining software to keep pace with the rate of change both in user requirements and in technological architectures such as user interfaces and implementation platforms.

1.3.2 There Is an Important Relationship Between Reuse and Software Process Maturity

Software process maturity is a measure of an organisation's capability to produce software to meet goals of quality, cost and schedule. Maturity increases to the extent that the software process becomes more repeatable, defined, managed, and subject to continual improvement. There are various approaches to measuring software process maturity: the best known is the Capability Maturity Model (CMM) for Software. Initiatives to increase the maturity of an organisation's software process are usually referred to under the umbrella term *software process improvement (SPI)*.

In the software domain, as in other business processes, *process* is conventionally distinguished from *technology*. Process means broadly *what* you do, and technology means broadly the technical practices that determine *how* the process is performed. Thus, the software process refers to activities such as product engineering, project management, quality assurance or configuration management, irrespective of the particular methods and tools (software technology) that may be selected to support those different parts of the process.

A mature process is one that is well managed and continually improving, independently of the technology used to support it. Of course, it is part of a well managed and continually improving process to be sure that appropriate technology is used; but judgments about maturity do not imply judgments about the appropriateness or otherwise of technology.

An important belief of the software process maturity movement is that a technology change on its own does not guarantee improvements in quality, cost, schedule or any other key indicator: the outcome is unpredictable, and change may even make things worse. That belief is clearly justified, for instance, by the relative failure of Computer Aided Software Engineering (CASE) technology. Even so, the more mature your process, the greater are your chances of ensuring that technology changes are assimilated successfully and profitably.

Reuse undoubtedly has a strong technology dimension, in the sense that it normally implies major changes in development and maintenance methods, and will probably need support from specialized tools. Technically oriented staff, such as programmers or software developers/ engineers, may see reuse primarily in such technological terms. But introducing systematic reuse is far more than a change in technology: it must be understood and managed in terms of a major set of changes to the software process. Two Chapters are devoted later in the book to process and management issues; the purpose here is no more than to introduce the essential process-related ideas into this introductory overview of systematic reuse. Those ideas are set out in *Fig. 1.6*.

Systematic reuse is a key practice within the overall software process, and must be treated in the same way as other key practices.

- Goals for reuse must be set.
- Commitment to reuse must be gained.
- Staff must be given the required abilities to perform reuse.
- The detailed activities involved in systematic reuse, and the corresponding work products, must be defined and documented.
- Means of reviewing and measuring the success of reuse must be defined and implemented.

The relationships between systematic reuse and other key practices must be considered, so that reuse becomes an integrated part of the complete process.

- Systematic reuse will impact other key practices, and vice versa. Consider the intimate relationships between reuse and (for instance) requirements management, project planning, configuration management, product engineering, and inspections (or peer reviews).

The relationship between systematic reuse introduction, and any corporate programme of software process improvement (SPI), should be carefully considered and understood.

Reuse does not play a great part in most software process maturity models. That means that, where such a model drives an organisation's SPI programme, there will not be a natural encouragement to include a reuse initiative as part of that programme. Different organisations may handle the relationship in different ways. The following are possible examples, all of which have been observed in practice.

- A SPI programme and a reuse programme may be regarded as distinct major initiatives, each sufficiently large and challenging to have its own goals and support organisation. This case may be described as 'parallel reuse and SPI'. There are two sub-cases, which may be called 'parallel coupled' and 'parallel disjoint', depending on the extent to which they are effectively integrated.
- Reuse may be identified as an improvement priority within an existing SPI programme. This case may be described as 'SPI-driven reuse'.
- Reuse may be identified as the initial driver for major change, and a reuse programme may be launched with little or no allowance made for the principles of successful SPI. If the organisation subsequently discovers and adopts the factors that underlie success in SPI, and ultimately embarks on a wider programme of SPI, this case may be described as 'reuse-driven SPI'. Otherwise it may be described as 'isolated reuse'.

Fig. 1.6 Reuse and the software process.

1.3.3 Reuse Is an Investment, Whether or Not You Call It That

Investment means giving up some benefit in the present, to produce some greater benefit in the future. Undertaking a programme of systematic reuse is undoubtedly an investment, although we may less readily think of it that way than in the case of more conventional investments in land, industrial plant and tools, buildings, skills, parts inventories, futures, standard manu-facturing designs, information and so on. The substantial and sustained management and technical effort involved in introducing reuse over a period of time has a cost, even if it is only the 'opportunity cost' of replacing effort that might otherwise yield more immediate returns; and that cost is incurred in the hope of larger returns in the future. Systematic reuse, as we have seen, involves developing a collection of reusable software assets. The very word *asset* is rich with overtones of investment.

More conventional investments are normally subject to careful and often sophisticated decision making, involving calculated estimates of net present value or payback period, and comparisons with competing investment proposals or with return on investment benchmarks. Actual investment costs are accounted for separately from costs incurred on current account; if benefits and savings can accurately be attributed to a specific investment, then a sound basis exists for computing the actual return on investment after a given period of time.

Software is seldom if ever regarded as an asset that carries value, either by management or in accountancy practice. There is seldom if ever any provi-sion for separating the costs incurred in developing software into investment costs and current costs, or even separating current costs into variable and overhead. Too often all software costs are simply lumped together as over-head. That is one important reason why return on investment figures for improvement initiatives (whether for reuse or for SPI in general) are rarely available and rarely credible.

But let us return to the point that, whether or not we are able to account for it as such, reuse is an investment. Investment unavoidably involves uncertainty, risk and forecasting the unknowable. Even if techniques for forecasting are used, and however smart they are, they cannot remove uncertainty or risk, and successful investment consequently often depends additionally on the subjective element of intuition or flair – characteristics of the entrepreneur. Deciding whether to invest in software in not just an exer-cise in technical and management analysis: in the end it also needs an element of entrepreneurial instinct.

1.3.4 Reuse May Be Pursued Within the Wider Business Context of Product Line Practice

While relatively new, software product line practice is rapidly attracting the attention of leading-edge software development organisations. According to a frequently used definition, a software product line is *a group of software products sharing a common managed set of features that satisfy specific needs of a selected market or mission.*

Product line practice seeks to leverage the potentially high-payoff technology of reuse by deploying it in the context of a well-defined business strategy and an appropriately modified software process. Application sectors in which PLP applications are to be found include the following:

- TV, VCR, DVD and audio;

- cell phones;

- digital cameras;

- printer peripherals;

- e-commerce systems;

- smart cards;

- geographic information system terminals;

- banking applications;

- telephone switch management and maintenance;

- medical imaging (magnetic resonance imaging, radiography, computer-aided tomography) and medical image archiving and communication;

- car supervision systems, including engine control, parking assistance, pre-crash applications, blind spot detection, autonomous parking, adaptive cruise control and integrated dashboards;

- diesel engine control, for trucks, buses, boats, railroad units, mining and farming equipment, etc.;

- ground vehicle simulators;

- command and control systems and simulators;

- fighter aircraft avionics;

- air traffic control;

- satellite attitude and orbit control;

- elevator control;

- pressure safety release valves and booster pumps.

The above list indicates that product line practice (PLP) is predominantly associated with the development of embedded software (often real-time) for industrial and defence systems and consumer products. There is a striking absence of representation of 'commercial' software, to support business processes or services, and of 'shrink-wrapped' or 'package' software.

PLP extends the reuse concept, of identifying commonalities and variations in software, upward to the products in which the software is embedded. The opportunities for software reuse influence the specification, design and economics of the products themselves, and vice versa. PLP handles commonalities and variabilities among products explicitly rather than accidentally. It should be requirements-driven, architecture-centric and components-based. A product line architecture is adaptable across the set of products constituting the product line, and should contain change and maximize reuse.

A product line aims to achieve large-grained reuse of assets, and rapid and inexpensive building of high-quality applications within the product line domain using the asset base. It must be able to evolve to incorporate new vendor technology and to provide new functionality required by customers. On their side customers may need to adjust their expectations to fit product line capabilities.

Making decisions about product lines requires understanding their implications on three dimensions: technical (product line architecture, development methods and tools etc.); organisational (team structure, operating models, individual roles and interfaces, communication etc.); business (business goals, divisional charters, market environment etc.).

PLP is driven by the 'produce, consume and customize' principle, which divides software development into two distinct life cycles: domain engineering (which *produces* reusable assets such as requirements, architectures and components, constituting a domain model that captures both the commonalities and the variabilities within the domain), and application engineering (which *consumes* and *customizes* assets to derive individual products within the domain).

Each software development project is important to an organisation, but the project for setting up a product line is far more important. It builds the basis for many specific development projects within the product line. It should be related to overall business and IT strategy, and look several years ahead.

1.4 Systematic Reuse – Crossing Frontiers

The purpose of this Section is to discuss systematic reuse as a critical point of transition in the history of computing, and to discuss why it has taken the software industry so long to achieve what has long been accepted common practice in other industries.

1.4.1 Systematic Reuse as a Critical Transition

We will look at systematic reuse first in the context of the 50-year-long history of software, and then in the context of the 10-year-long history of software process improvement.

Software started in 1948, in the UK. In that year the Manchester 'Baby' was the first machine to demonstrate the execution of stored-program instructions. The following year, in Cambridge, EDSAC was the first stored-program machine to execute a complete program producing 'real-world' results. From the start, the EDSAC group was using subroutines, which can be regarded as an early form of reuse. Reuse was there at the very beginning.

Since then, there has been a continuous stream of innovations that have pushed forward the frontiers of reuse. They include such things as assembly codes, high-level languages, macro-assemblers, code generators, customizable packages, class libraries, test-pack generators and so on. A characteristic of those innovations is that they have been largely on the supply side. They have enabled computer manufacturers and other suppliers to package reusable assets (such as very small chunks of functionality, in the case of high-level languages) in such a way as to raise the plateau on which application developers work, and thus to reduce their workload. Of course, these innovations have been indispensable to the progress of computing, which would have been impossible without them.

On the user side, however, application developers have largely been limited to ad hoc reuse, almost entirely at the code level, using the facilities (subroutines, macros, classes, copy-and-paste, and so on) provided by manufacturers and other vendors. The promise of systematic reuse is that it will enable reuse to 'jump the species barrier' (like mad cow disease!) from the supplier side to the developer side, and bring about the very large improvements in quality, productivity and business benefit that are necessary and possible. That point of crossover, at which we may now be standing, may prove to be a critical frontier in the 50-year history of software, during all of which time reuse has been trying to break through to its full potential.

Let us now turn to the history of software process improvement (SPI), which effectively spans a much shorter period of about 10 years. As we saw earlier in this Chapter, the driving concept in SPI has been process maturity, which simply assesses the degree to which processes are institutionalized, independently of the technical practices which constitute the real fabric of the processes. As we presently understand and use it, SPI offers great benefits in raising us from the swamp of level 1 chaos; but nevertheless it has inherent limitations. Radical progress will come not just from managing the process better, irrespective of its substance, but from improving both substance and management together. Systematic reuse offers arguably the most promising means of improving the substance of the process; pursued in parallel with SPI, it offers exciting prospects of transforming software capability to an extent that SPI could not achieve unaided.

1.4.2 Why So Long?

It may thus be that systematic software reuse by application developers is an idea whose time has finally come. Why, however, has it taken so long? Reuse can be described simply as not reinventing the wheel. The need and the benefits of not reinventing the wheel are understood in all areas of human activity, and much successful ingenuity has been devoted over centuries to achieving that goal. The result has been that as a species we have made progress (according to the saying) by 'standing on our predecessors' shoulders and not their toes'. Except in software. Why?

As a familiar example of reuse, consider automobiles. When developing a new model, a manufacturer may well decide to retain an engine design used in one or more earlier models. The decision whether or not to do so will be influenced by questions such as whether the power production and fuel consumption of the existing engine meet the objectives defined for the new car, and whether its shape fits the new layout.

According to the answers to such questions, it may be possible to use the existing engine design without adaptation. On the other hand, it may turn out that some change is necessary. In that case, further questions will arise about the extent of the adaptations, and how much (for instance) they will incur heavy costs in redesigning the engine production line.

That kind of scenario occurs equally for other parts of a car. It also occurs across other manufactured products, across production plant (such as assembly lines or oil refineries), and across the construction industry. It extends further still, beyond the production of physical artefacts, to commercial services (such as financial products or telecommunications services), internal business processes (such as contracting or double-entry accounting) and information formats (such as application forms or tabloid newspaper layouts).

It is important to recognize what are being reused in all these cases. They are generalized abstractions – designs, methods, plans, formats – not the specific instances which eventually embody those abstractions. To return to the car engine, it is the design that is reused, by being transferred from one model to another. Reusing an individual physical engine is quite a different thing, and occurs when a second-hand dealer transfers an engine from one car that is to be scrapped to another that is to be sold!

Much is conventionally made of the unique nature of software, and the difference between software and other products. Software, it is said, is abstract, and its production is a design-intensive process. As we have seen, however, reuse normally means precisely the reuse of design-like abstractions. 'Not reinventing the wheel' means not reinventing the concept of the wheel, rather than a specific instance of a wheel. The supposed uniqueness of software does not thus appear to be a terribly good justification for its slow take-up of reuse.

The real difference between software and other products and processes in business is probably a cultural one, which arises from the nature of the product, but which has had very destructive consequences for the management of the process. There are more technical degrees of freedom throughout the development of a software product than exist for other arte-facts. Non-software artefacts are constrained by natural laws and the known capacities of the human brain, which reduce the technical options open to designers. It is possible, in contrast, to approach each new software product as a blank sheet, awaiting the full range of the designer's creative inspiration.

A software culture has been allowed to develop in which designers tend to regard their task in just that way, as one of creative inspiration, rather like (for example) artists. Instinctively, they tend to look down on reuse, just as a 'serious' novelist might look down on those authors of cheap romantic fiction who construct storylines out of standard elements. The (not invented here) NIH syndrome is alive and flourishing throughout the software industry, and it is encouraged to thrive by the degrees of freedom that are technically available.

It has also been allowed to thrive by weak management, who generally have had little understanding of the economics of software production, who fail to adapt and apply normal practices of good management, and who are blinded with technicalities by specialists seeking to preserve their vested interests.

Thus reinventing the wheel in software has gone on, and on, and on. We may hope, and indeed with some help from this book, it will not, perhaps, go on much longer.

1.5 A Note on the Experience Base Used in This Book

An important source for the writing of this book has been the real-world experience, elicited through interviews, of a number of organizations that have experimented with introducing reuse into their software development practice. Most of the points made in the book are illustrated by means of *experience notes*, drawn from that repository of practical experience. The repository represents experiences of reuse as seen through the eyes of the people who have really done it. They are the people who know best what they have done, what their successes and problems were, and the business setting into which reuse was introduced. The experience base is an informal summary of these people's stories, of how it seemed to them.

Of the companies that contributed to the experience base, it proved possible to obtain information about four in more depth. These depth studies were used as the basis for comparative case histories, that are presented in parallel in Chapters 8 and 9. These four companies have permitted their identities to be used, and they are referred to by name in both the experience notes and in the case histories: they are Chase Computer Services (UK), ELIOP (Spain), Sodalia (Italy) and Thomson-CSF (France). The other companies remain anonymous.

Reference

1. Reed, D. (1995) Tools for Software Reuse. *Object Magazine* (Feb. 1995).

Reusable Software Assets

2

ABSTRACT

The concept of reusable software assets is central to software reuse. If we consider reuse as a way of capturing and exploiting business experise, the word 'asset' is seen to be very appropriate. Software assets encapsulate business knowledge and are high value for a company. This Chapter defines what assets are, explains what makes them reusable and describes their life-cycle.

2.1 What Is a Software Asset?

Let's start by defining the word 'asset'.

Definition

Reusable assets are composed of a collection of related software work products that may be reused from one application to another. In this book, the word 'component' is used with a specific meaning: a software component is an *executable* asset that may be integrated *as-is* into an application. A component is a specific type of asset that refers to component-based technologies.

In this Chapter, we will deliberately omit the qualifier 'reusable' and just talk about software assets, focusing on reusable ones.

Software-based systems are critical to the business, but business knowledge and business process definitions are often buried in computer programs. Assets are important, not only because they can be reused, but also because they capture business knowledge. A company developing software should attach the same importance to software assets as to any other kind of assets (financial, real estate . . .). Developing applications reusing existing business-oriented assets is a way to partition skills and to be protected from staff turnover.

2.1.1 A Software Asset Is a Software Product

Every software asset must be considered as an internal software product and its creator as a software editor. All the functions of a software editor must be carried out in order to manage assets efficiently (Table 2.1).

2.1.2 What Kind of Asset?

Vertical assets are specific to an application domain (*Fig. 2.1*). They are the most valuable assets since they capture the business knowledge that is specific to an organization and they represent the organization's know-how and its competitive advantage.

Table 2.1 An asset is a product.

Product definition	The need for an asset must be evaluated before its creation. Its cost should be evaluated and compared to its value added in relation to the potential users.
Product industrialization	The asset must be tested, documented and packaged. Otherwise it will not be reusable.
Advertisement	The asset must be disseminated and advertised. People must be aware of its existence and must be convinced of its interest.
Pre-sale	Assistance during the evaluation phase must be provided in order that the reuser does not lose time trying to understand the asset.
Maintenance and support	The reuser must be assisted when using the asset. It is not his/her task to modify the asset in case of corrective or evolutionary maintenance. Reusers must be notified when a new version is released.
Follow-up	Feedback from (re)users must be collected in order to capitalize on and improve existing assets.

- Financial object models
- C++ libraries of financial instruments
- Design and code for a customer management module
- Design and code for a patient management module (healthcare)
- A geophysical calculation algorithm
- A generic object model in the Air Traffic Control domain
- A framework for SCADA(Supervision, Control and Data Acquisition) applications

Fig. 2.1 Examples of vertical assets.

Horizontal assets are easier to identify and reuse because they represent recurrent architectural elements. They can be reused independently of the application domain, the main constraint being that the application architectural choices must be compatible with the asset. We can distinguish technical assets, which are technically necessary to implement low layers of a software system, from generic assets, which provide generic services useful to more than a single application domain (*Fig. 2.2*).

Note that this differentiation is subjective. An asset may be considered as vertical within a domain. But if this domain is split into finer domains, the assets may be shared, and thus become horizontal.

This is mainly due to the fact that domains may be nested. It is possible to define very precise domains (e.g. network performance management, invoicing . . .) that belong to more general domains (e.g. network management; administration . . .). In this case some assets may appear horizontal, even if they are specific to business administration.

Technical assets
- GUI objects (forms, spreadsheet tables, . . .)
- Container classes, data structures, basic algorithms
- Database access libraries
- Network communication libraries

Generic assets
- Reporting service
- Authentication service
- Trace and log service
- Error management framework

Fig. 2.2 Examples of horizontal assets.

To avoid this indistinct situation, domains must be defined as precisely as possible (even if they are grouped into higher level domains), and be consistent with the company's business.

Experience Note

> In the SURPRISE experience database, all but one of the companies that are organized for reuse do not limit the scope of reuse to horizontal assets but address business-oriented assets.

2.1.3 Asset Granularity

Assets may have very different sizes and granularities. For instance:

- a function or a procedure;
- a class;
- a group of classes;
- a subsystem, a framework or a service;
- an application or a product.

Assets are often nested (an asset contains several assets). The reuser is free to reuse the overall asset or one of its nested assets.

The bigger the asset is, the earlier it should be taken into account in the application development process.

2.1.4 What Is an Asset Made of?: The Asset Model

A reusable asset is potentially made of many life-cycle products:

- requirements definition;
- architecture definition;
- analysis models;
- design models and code;

- test programs;

- test scenarios;

- test reports.

A single asset is made of a set of related work products. These work products can represent the same piece of software at different abstraction levels (requirements, analysis, design, code, tests), and thus each work-product of the asset can be reused at each step of the life-cycle (before and after coding). For instance, test programs are highly reusable.

Do not limit reuse to code reuse. All work products may be reused at each life cycle step.

Experience Note

A telecommunication devices manufacturer is extensively reusing test cases to validate equipment conformity to different national standards. The same test cases are applied to different equipments.

A billing and accounting applications editor built a test cases repository in order to automate the validation of different versions of a product.

The reusable material must also be packaged with all the information necessary to reuse it (asset 'meta-information', or asset description (Karlsson, 1995)):[1]

- classification information to facilitate rapid retrieval of suitable assets;

- description to facilitate understanding of what the asset does;

- documentation to facilitate understanding of how to use it (and if necessary to customize it);

- qualification and test information to facilitate evaluating and testing it;

- information about its origin to facilitate obtaining support or additional information.

All these characteristics are summarized in the object model (using UML notation) of *Fig. 2.3.*

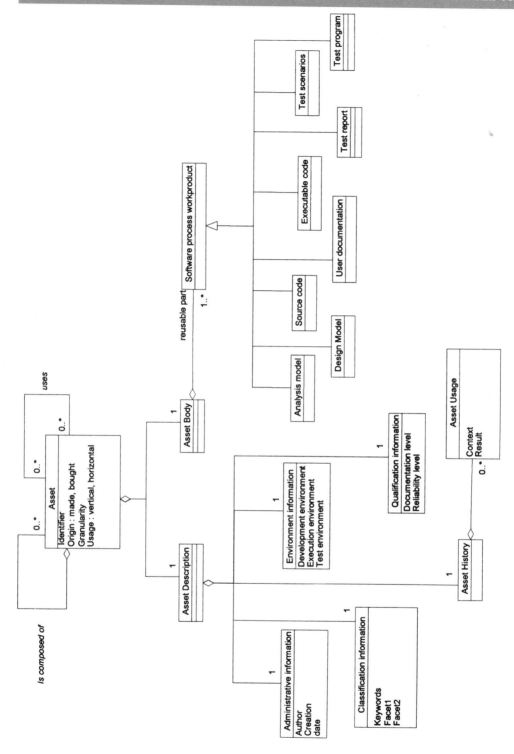

Fig. 2.3 The asset model.

This model shows that an asset is made of two kinds of information: its body (containing reusable work products) and its description (containing all the information necessary to support the reuse process). Qualification and classification information (in particular the notion of 'facet') refers to the related processes and is detailed respectively in Section 2.2 (characteristics of reusable assets) of this Chapter and in Chapter 3 (reuse repository). The concept of asset history is discussed in Section 2.3 of this Chapter.

This model also shows the nestedness of assets and the fact that assets may have other kinds of relationships: for instance an asset can use another asset. Each company should define its own asset model according to how reuse is intended to be practised. As illustrated by the above example, an asset model should define the following.

- Asset body.

- Asset description (i.e. information necessary to support reuse processes).

- Asset documentation.

- The asset's relationships with other assets. The above model shows that there are two main kinds of relationships between assets.

  - Composition relationships: as mentioned above, assets may be nested. An asset may be composed of other reusable assets. The reuser then has the choice of reusing the overall composite asset (including all its component assets) or just one of its finer-grained components.

  - Usage relationships: a given asset can use functionalities of existing assets. In this case the asset reuser will have to decide whether also to reuse related assets or whether to provide a new implementation of them. In particular a vertical asset may use technical assets (GUI objects, middleware) for implementation purposes.

  - The asset's construction, validation and execution environment.

Experience Note

From the SURPRISE experience base, we can identify reuse success factors related to the kind of asset considered. All companies that have unquestionably succeeded in reuse have common asset features.

- **Consider both horizontal and vertical assets**. The former are easier to define but the latter are critical to the business.

- **Use of large-grained assets** (libraries, frameworks, domain models . . .), rather than fine-grained ones (classes, procedures . . .). They are more efficient and ensure higher leverage.

- Reusing large-grained assets also ensures a common architecture between applications. **Applications architectures** should be strongly influenced by the assets they are reusing.

- A lot of small assets are difficult to manage and identify. Thus, it is more efficient to **manage a reduced number of critical business** assets shared at corporate or department level.

- **Assets contain many lifecycle work products.** Coding represents less than 25 per cent of a system development cost, and thus reuse must not be limited to this activity.

2.1.5 Technical Strategies

Assets may have different shapes. The shape determines the way an asset is implemented and the way it will be used and reused. Here is a list (see Table 2.2) of different possible strategies (neither exhaustive nor mutually exclusive) for implementing assets.

Experience Note

As already discussed, reuse is fitted to product line development. Thomson Airsys ATM is a company that develops **Air Traffic Control** systems for different airports all over the world. Rather than building a complete framework, they analysed their business and their domain (ATC). As a result they manage a product baseline which is a repository containing 'the best compromise between commonalities and variabilities' of the product line. This means that on the one hand, for efficiency reasons, all software pieces corresponding to specific (and rare) cases are not kept in the baseline, but on the other hand the baseline must not be reduced to a low common factor between individual products, because otherwise reuse opportunities (features that are common to two or more systems but not to all of them) may be missed. Each new product version is built by extracting useful software pieces from the product baseline. Software pieces include many lifecycle products (from requirements to test cases). Of course, this requires that the baseline is very well organized and changes are controlled. The baseline is periodically updated according to recent releases. Such an approach enables Airsys ATM to achieve reuse levels close to 90 per cent.

Table 2.2 Type of asset.

Type of asset	Description	Type of usage
Executable component	It may execute separately. Applications reuse it by invoking it or calling its services at run-time.	Invoke
Library	A set of classes or procedures that may be integrated to and called from several applications.	Integrate
Pattern	They consist in identified modelling solutions that may be applied to several problems when modelling different systems.	Imitate
Frameworks	Applications are built customizing and adapting the framework in accordance to its architectural style and rules.	Customize
Domain models	They constitute the baseline on which any application (inside this domain) model is built.	Build from
Software packages	The simplest way to reuse is to integrate existing design and code work products.	Integrate
Application generator	It makes it possible to build a new application, or a part of it, from its specifications.	Generate
Requirement models	The requirement model, on which a product has been built, may be kept and compared to new customers' requirements in order to evaluate if the product can fulfil their need.	Compare
Product baseline	It consists of all stable software work-products that are contained in different versions of a product. Any new product is built from all or some of these software pieces.	Extract

2.2 What Are the Characteristics of Reusable Assets?

Obviously an asset is not very valuable if it is not intended to be reused. But not every piece of software is reusable. The qualification process (see also Section 4.3, in the Chapter on reuse processes) determines asset reusability according to pre-defined criteria.

2.2.1 General Criteria: Quality and Reusability

Any asset aiming at being reused should respect certain general criteria.

- Compliance to standards, guidelines and rules concerning design, coding, documentation (e.g. usage of documentation templates, naming policies . . .).

- Compliance of asset engineering process to standard and best practices: respect of engineering phases, documenting and tracing each step, respect of design methods, respect of test and validation process etc.

- Completeness of artefacts and information provided, and conformity to asset model.

- Simplicity and understandability.

- Modularity.

2.2.2 Functional Criteria

Functional criteria mainly concern vertical assets. Since they are very specific to each domain, we can only give the general functional characteristics of any asset.

- A vertical asset's function is to automate or simulate, fully or partially, a business process.

- A vertical asset provides services and is able to prioritise requests, schedule and record their execution.

- A vertical asset must always remain available to its clients and must be able to process parallel activities.

- A vertical asset can delegate services to nested assets or to other assets.

- Vertical assets must comply to standards in effect in the considered domain.

- Assets must implement a trade-off between being too specific (and less reusable) and being too generic (and less valuable). A way to avoid this dilemma is to make the asset customizable. It is the purpose of domain analysis (see Chapter 4 on reuse processes) to determine an asset's variability.

A company should define other functional criteria that are specific to a particular domain.

2.2.3 Technical Criteria

In order to be easily reused and integrated, assets should respect the following technical characteristics.

Interoperability: ability to communicate easily with other assets (that may be implemented with different languages, that may run on different machines with different platforms . . .), and thus to be integrated into an application.

Portability: ability to run on different platforms. In particular a vertical asset (the function of which is not related to a given implementation platform) should not be directly connected to implementation services such as GUIs or databases. Logical interfaces to these services should be provided in order to ensure the portability and independence of business-related software from computer implementation.

Differentiation between **interface and implementation**: how an asset is used (or reused) and how it is implemented are two different things that should not be mixed, since they can evolve separately.

Composition: assets can be grouped to form higher-level assets and can be decomposed into fine-grained assets. Assets must respect reusability criteria at any level.

Self-descriptiveness: an executable asset, manipulated as a black box, must describe its own interface. It must provide its own 'usage protocol'. The user is then able to understand, without consulting the asset's engineering work products, its interface and properties.

Location transparency: executable components may run on different machines, without impacting the rest of the system.

Security: since the component contains executable code and is reused as a black box among a community of software developers, the reuser must be able to control the origin of the asset (digital signatures), and the asset's access to private resources.

Plug and play: component portability is required not at construction time but at run time. For instance, a single piece of Java code may be executed on different platforms.

The last four criteria may be applicable to any type of asset but have a specific meaning in the context of component-based technologies such as Java Beans or ActiveX. Such technologies make it possible to build applications from black-box executable components. Existing run-time (i.e.

executable) components are manipulated at construction time: they contain active code. Refer to Chapter 7 (Reuse Techniques and Technologies) for more detailed information on how existing technologies can support these technical criteria.

2.3 Managing Software Assets

2.3.1 Asset Life Cycle

Assets are alive! They will take part in several applications and thus will be managed for a long period of time. Thus, we can identify two main axes of variability for an asset.

- Variability through time: the asset is maintained, corrected and enhanced to correspond to evolving requirements.

- Variability across applications: the asset may be adapted according to the different applications that use it.

Figure 2.4 illustrates the possible states in an asset's life, from its identification (at this moment it is not developed yet) to its validation (certification), classification and publication to all teams. Then the asset will be reused and maintained.

Figure 2.4 may be considered as a workflow process, each state of the asset life involving different actors. It is often interesting to trace the information related to an asset's life and, in particular, to each time it is reused. This is the meaning of the 'asset history' that appeared in the asset model in a previous sub-section. Each attempt to reuse an asset should be recorded (Karlsson, 1995)[1], together with the context in which it was reused, the qualitative and possibly quantitative results (success or failure, judgement on the asset, modification required, time spent, time saved . . .).

- Do not consider assets as 'rooted' pieces of software that are not supposed to evolve.

- Keep track of assets' **usage histories**: this is a way to facilitate measurements, to give confidence in an asset to potential reusers, and to notify an asset's users when a new version of the asset is released.

2.3.2 Organizing Asset Acquisition

A company or project must consider several options if an asset is needed that does not already exist.

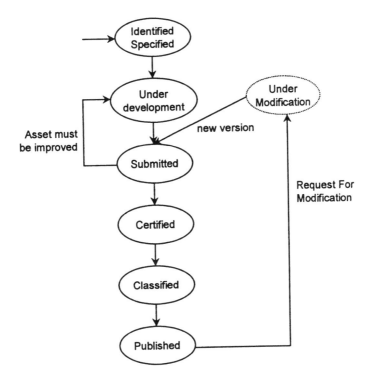

Fig. 2.4 States of an asset.

- Purchase it if a suitable commercial off-the-shelf (COTS) product exists.

- Search for a free asset on the internet or in public archives.

- Develop it.

- Subcontract its development to a software house.

The software component market is not yet completely organized but is strongly emerging. Several vendors are building component offerings instead of turnkey software products. There is more and more quality public domain software available. This situation is mainly due to two factors: internet/web development, and the emergence of frameworks and component technologies that make it possible to plug components into standard environments.

Externally acquired software must follow a process that is similar to internally acquired assets.

- Search for existing and useful assets.

- Evaluation of candidate assets.

- Customization and packaging of a selected acquired asset according to company standards.

- Documentation of the asset (if the documentation is lacking, or to specify the way the asset must be used).

- Dissemination of the asset.

- Support and maintenance: if a COTS asset is to be used by several projects, its support and maintenance should be centralized in a single team (which is in contact with the source of external support).

Experience Note

In the SURPRISE experience base, about half of the companies envisage internal reuse only, the other half already perform external acquisition of COTS assets. In the second case, COTS assets are considered as part of the reuse program because, although they are for the moment generally limited to horizontal assets, acquisition of business assets is seriously considered for the future. In the first case, of those that do not invest in COTS reuse, the main roadblock resides in the reluctance to use the Internet, which is the main vector for disseminating COTS assets, but which is not judged to provide enough guarantees in terms of security, confidentiality, or trustworthiness of COTS providers and COTS assets.

2.3.3 Make or Buy?

Buying COTS assets is becoming a more and more serious option to consider. Deciding to develop or to buy thus becomes a critical issue. The following table (Table 2.3) summarizes some decision rules.

Table 2.3 Make, buy or subcontract: decision grid.

Question / issue to consider	Alternatives / possible answers	Consequences
1. Availability of external products	YES: Expected products seem available (commercially or public domain).	COTS strategy is possible. Evaluation of candidate assets is necessary. • BUY (cf. 2 to 8)
	NO: such products do not exist on the market.	COTS strategy is not possible. • MAKE or SUBCTR (cf. 2, 3, 5, 6, 7, 9)
2. Commercial exploitation of acquired assets	Commercial usage is allowed.	The asset may be integrated into commercial products. Check deployment conditions. • BUY (cf. 3 to 8)
	Asset is available for internal or pedagogic usage only.	Cannot be used as-is but may be a model to develop an owned asset • MAKE or SUBCTR (cf 5, 6, 7, 9)
	Too many deployment constraints (cost, licences . . .).	• MAKE or SUBCTR (cf 5, 6, 7, 9)
3. Asset evolution	The asset will have to evolve importantly, in a not-predictable way.	Risky if the acquired asset is not mastered. • MAKE (cf. 5, 9)
	Small and predictable evolutions.	• BUY (cf. 4 to 8)
4. Asset shape	Quality source and documentation available.	• BUY (cf. 5 to 8)
	Full black-box.	Risky if the asset need to be adapted (cf. 3). • MAKE (cf. 5, 9)
5. Availability of resources and skills required to develop assets	Low availability.	A minimum of resources are necessary to master the asset. The asset owner is in charge of Evaluation, Customization, Support and Maintenance of the asset. • BUY or SUBCTR (cf. 6, 7, 8)
	Highly available.	• MAKE (cf. 9)
6. Certification constraints	I will not be able to meet my high certification constraints if my final product integrates external software.	• MAKE (cf. 9)
	No specific constraints.	Normal purchase process is possible. • BUY(cf. 7, 8)

Table 2.3 continued

Question / issue to consider	Alternatives / possible answers	Consequences
7. Strategy / Ownership	The final product is highly strategic and I need to completely master my product.	● MAKE (cf. 9)
	No specific constraints.	I should not invest too many resources and skills in this domain. ● BUY or SUBCTR (cf. 8)
8. Trustability	I cannot completely trust the provider.	It is not a problem if the product is acquired with source code and if there is an investment to customize and master the product. Otherwise, asset cannot be acquired. ● MAKE (cf 9)
	I consider I can depend on this provider.	● BUY or SUBCTR
9. Time to market	I absolutely need to reduce time to market.	● BUY or SUBCTR
	I accept the foreseen time to market.	● MAKE
SUBCTR: Sub-contract.		

Experience Note

The SURPRISE experience base shows that many different types of software artefacts are reused. Companies that practise ad hoc reuse (the majority) just **duplicate code** on a case by case basis. This solution is not satisfactory because software is not shared by the whole software community within the company but by a small group of developers. Moreover this solution does not allow common maintenance of the reused pieces of code. These pieces of code will rapidly diverge as software evolves.

With systematic reuse, software assets are generally stored as aggregations of (for example) **analysis, design models, documentation, code and test cases**. Traditionally, *libraries* ensure black box reuse thanks to their API. Companies also elaborate *business domain models* that constitute a reference and a starting point for all applications within a model, ensuring consistency. Others focus on *technical assets* that are generally easier to identify and to reuse (e.g. GUI components). But more 'accomplished' forms of reuse have proved to be possible.

- New technologies (Corba, Java Beans, ActiveX) allow *component-based development* (refer to Chapter 7 on reuse technology). Executable components are stored and manipulated by development tools in order to be integrated into applications.

- *Frameworks* make it possible to reuse an architecture (together with the code that implements it) and to specialize it for a given context. Example: Sodalia, an Italian telecommunications software company, provides network management systems. For this purpose, frameworks have been developed. These frameworks have been instantiated to create several systems for different customers. They can be customized to different customer situations: different kinds of telecommunications equipment and protocols, different kind of measurements on this equipment, different deployment architectures (portability and scalability). Such frameworks require significant development effort but are one of the most advanced ways to achieve reuse.

We also found more uncommon forms of achieving reuse.

- A systems engineering company practising reuse at system requirements level: customer requirements are captured and compared to existing product features in a repository. Systems engineers are thus able to determine which version of which product is closest to the customer's need, and what is the required level of customization.

- As already mentioned, for some software companies the main reusable assets are test cases.

- A company in the field of telecommunications puts the emphasis on *COTS assets*. See the next experience note on COTS reuse.

Experience Note

As already mentioned half of the companies studied actually reuse COTS assets, and most consider this solution as an emerging issue to be seriously considered. However, this option mainly concerns horizontal assets, until the vertical COTS market becomes really mature, and in most cases COTS reuse is not performed in the framework of a formalized process as is the case for internal asset reuse. In most cases, every project buys libraries according to its current needs, without capitalizing them at corporate level.

The exception to this observation comes from Sodalia, where there is a real investment in the COTS asset acquisition process. One member of the Reuse Support Organization (RSO) is dedicated to identifying and evaluating useful products on the market. There are two possible scenarios: in both cases, the process is driven by the RSO specialist.

- There is an identified short-term need for a given COTS asset coming from at least one project. In this case, the asset is acquired, qualified, extensively tested, and customized according to the way that projects are going to use it and in order to integrate it into the development infrastructure. If necessary, the external asset is documented, in order to fill a possible lack of documentation or in order to document the way it has been customized and any recommendations for its usage within the company. Then the asset is published in the corporate asset repository, together with internally developed assets. Any project that requires it is able to access it, evaluate it against the project's specific needs, reuse it, and benefit from support from the reuse team which has already gone though the appropriation process and which centralizes technical support (calling the COTS vendor's technical support when necessary). When the client project decides to integrate the COTS asset within its application, it must check rights and licensing with the reuse team, which is the only contact point with the COTS vendor.

- The asset is judged valuable and useful for the company, but there is no project that is a potential customer in the short term. In this case, the candidate COTS asset is anyway qualified and evaluated by the reuse team (generally using an evaluation version). It is not purchased until the first user is identified, but it is already considered as a company asset, for which the appropriation process has been done. It is registered and described in the corporate repository as a COTS asset without 'body' but which can be purchased as soon as a user is identified. This is what Sodalia calls a 'virtual asset'.

For more information on COTS assets, and on examples of accessible COTS asset repositories on the internet, consult Chapter 3 (reuse repository).

2.4 Assets vs Objects

What is the relationship between assets and objects, between reuse and object-oriented technology? It seems appropriate to discuss this controversial question here, whereas further considerations on technologies are detailed in Chapter 7.

2.4.1 OO Is Neither Necessary Nor Sufficient

Applying OO technology is neither necessary nor sufficient for the practice of reuse. Reuse may be based on other technologies, and reusable artefacts need not be objects (see Experience Note). Moreover usage of OO technology, in itself, does not guarantee a good level of reuse.

OO technology is one factor that positively influences reusability: it drives designers toward (but does not guarantee) reusability. However, reusability alone does not ensure successful reuse: lots of non-technical aspects need to be considered (organization, culture . . .). There are many reasons why a very good asset may never be reused.

2.4.2 OO Is an 'Enabling' Factor

Migration to OO technology brings a positive context to reuse introduction. Many companies take advantage of the organizational and technical changes implied by such migration to introduce a reuse policy. Furthermore, objects facilitate reuse implementation, in particular the construction and integration of assets.

A business asset is an integral set of data, processing, business rules, properties and constraints. Business objects encapsulate all these elements, and they offer a good way to implement consistent and evolutionary business assets.

The object approach leads to less monolithic systems than in the past, and prompts designers to implement three-tier architectures. This kind of architecture facilitates the identification and integration of reusable assets (business objects, user interface components, etc.). Three-tier architectures enable developers to build pieces of software that are specialized for one task (business logic, user interface, data access, middleware . . .).

Finally, object principles such as encapsulation, aggregation, classification and polymorphism offer flexibility when designing assets, and constitute basic principles for patterns and frameworks that are strong reuse enablers.

Experience Note

Within the SURPRISE experience database, among companies that have a reuse programme, underlying technologies are very variable. About one-third exclusively use object modelling and languages (often CC++), about one-third exclusively use traditional approaches (such as C modules or 4GLs) or Ada, and the remainder use both approaches on different projects.

One of the most frequently observed risk and failure factors resides in the fact that many companies fully rely on object technologies to achieve reuse. Sometimes, new technologies are introduced and reuse is expected without addressing other issues like organization, roles and processes. As stated above, these technologies may be an enabling factor, but they are not sufficient. In the case of migration to new technologies, obtaining reuse is generally one step beyond the technology adoption and it requires additional changes.

2.4.3 What About Business Objects?

Business objects are objects (in the OO sense) that represent a concept manipulated by a company in the frame of its business activity (*Fig. 2.5*). They are highly reusable vertical assets.

Business objects have several properties:

- attributes that represent business data;

- links to other objects that represent business interactions;

The Object Management Group (OMG), the industrial consortium in charge of standardization of object technologies, has set up task forces on vertical services definition ('vertical domain-specific interfaces') and business objects. In fact the Business Object Domain Task Force (BODTF) is currently defining a technical platform (a framework) into which business objects can be plugged.

The vertical domain-specific interfaces define business-specific services as class interfaces (using IDL, the OMG's Interface Definition Language). The domains addressed include: imagery, information superhighways, accounting, oil exploration and production, distributed simulation, computer-integrated manufacturing, process control, and computer-aided design. For more information, refer to (OMG)[3] and (BOTDF)[4].

Fig. 2.5 Business objects at the OMG.

- operations or services that represent business logic;

- constraints that represent business rules.

Business objects are identified during an OO domain analysis activity (refer to Chapter 4 on processes) or during a traditional object analysis. Practically, a business object represents a single concept (a client, a product, a financial instrument . . .) but is often modelled as a group of consistent classes and implemented as a component.

Most specialists distinguish at least two main kinds of business objects (Taylor, 1995)[2].

- Objects that represent business entities or resources (e.g. Client, Employee, Product, Financial Instrument, Network Equipment, Bank Account, Invoice . . .). Such objects are responsible for managing resources, cost, availability and planning.

- Objects that represent business processes (Invoicing, Manufacturing, Sales, Inventory, Purchasing . . .). They support the execution of a process and manage its objectives, its progress, its costs and the use of necessary resources.

References

1. Karlsson, E.A. (1995) *Software Reuse, a Holistic Approach.* John Wiley & Sons.
2. Taylor, D. (1995) *Business Engineering with Object Technology.* John Wiley & Sons.
3. Object Management Group (OMG): http://www.omg.org
4. BODTF: OMG Business Object Domain Task Force: http://www.dataaccess.com/bodtf/omg.org.htm.

Reuse Repository 3

ABSTRACT

The repository is the place where reusable software assets are stored, along with the catalogue of assets. Everybody should be aware that it contains important company know-how, and should be able to access and use it easily. In this Chapter we take the point of view of a technical manager charged with setting up the reuse repository for her company. First we describe the repository in terms of the functions it should offer. Then we examine some families of tools on the market that offer these functions.

3.1 Who Needs a Repository?

The first question to be asked is probably: does a company invariably need a central repository and, if not, what are the conditions in which a repository is required? A company or a development team can afford not to have a defined and managed repository for assets provided that the developers are able, even in its absence, to know what assets exist and where they are. This situation is not normal and could be summed up as one where both the number of people and the number of assets are very limited. In general, the factors to be considered in setting up a repository are:

- the number of developers, development teams and development sites in the company;

- the number of assets, and the number of different domains to which the assets belong.

As these numbers grow, assets have to be managed in an organized and defined way. An essential part of this management effort is to define and maintain a catalogue of assets. This will avoid the situation in which developers do not know about (a) an existing asset that would match part of their need, (b) where to look for this asset or who owns it, and (c) what to do with a new potentially reusable asset.

A repository to store assets offers the following advantages:

- the definition and common recognition of a place for assets, therefore a known and unique place to look for and deposit assets;

- a homogeneous way of documenting, searching and accounting for assets;

- a defined way of managing changes and enhancements to assets, including configuration management procedures.

3.2 Requirements for a Reuse Repository

3.2.1 What Is Stored Inside a Repository?

As defined in Chapter 2, assets have a description and a body. The asset body is, in general, composed of related work products (for instance a design description, the related source and object code in programming language A, the related source and object code in programming language B, the related test cases). The asset description has a number of attributes (at least a unique name, an author, a creation or upgrade date, a set of keywords or facet values) that make it possible to identify, describe and search for it.

Figure 2.4 in Chapter 2 presented the asset model, or how a single asset is decomposed. Figure 3.1 extends that model by considering a set of assets. This requires adding the concepts of *repository* and *catalogue*. A repository is composed of two parts: one catalogue and a set of assets. The catalogue is composed of a set of asset descriptions. So a repository broadly comprises all the assets in an organization, together with their catalogue. The catalogue comprises, as will be explained later, an organized collection of asset descriptions, and the related searching and management services.

An essential piece of information in an asset description is where the asset body is located within the repository. The work-products that comprise the body of an asset are usually stored in a file system, or in a configuration management system, and this will be our working hypothesis.

50

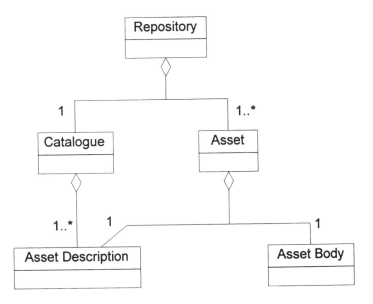

Fig. 3.1 The repository model.

With the above definitions we can understand more easily the difference between a managed reuse repository and a non-managed one. Both store the work products that compose an asset, but the non-managed one lacks both the catalogue and the concept of a reusable asset, i.e. the fact that a set of work products compose a meaningful piece of information to be treated and reused as a whole. Clearly, without the notion of asset the burden of finding and assembling work products is on the shoulders of the potential reuser. Without the catalogue, the potential reuser has also the burden of finding one asset among a number that may be available. Such obstacles would inevitably be a barrier to reuse.

A repository can also contain *virtual assets*. Virtual assets are assets where only the description exists without the body. Virtual assets are used to signal that an asset is known to be either available or required, but will be produced or bought later, usually just before it will be used for the first time.

3.2.2 Functions of a Repository

In a few words, a reuse repository should be able to identify assets, associate a description to each of them, and maintain links to the work products that contribute to its body. In detail, a repository could offer the following functions. Note that not all the functions listed are required, depending on the context and needs of the organization using the repository.

Asset identification and description. Each asset should be identified in a homogeneous way. For instance an asset could be identified by a unique name, and described by a standard set of attributes. It is important to establish and maintain a common interface to assets, so that all members of the software organization become familiar with it. Some attributes (e.g. domain or sub-domain of the asset, category or functionality offered, etc.) are essential to classify and retrieve the asset.

Asset insertion. A user (typically the reuse manager) should be able to insert a new asset in the repository. This means storing the asset body and inserting a corresponding new asset description in the catalogue. Insertion in the catalogue is strictly linked with determining the classification of the asset (see the 'Organization and search' function, below). A variation of the insertion function is the insertion of a new version of an asset body.

Catalogue browsing. A user should be able to browse the catalogue to access the description of assets. This function is sufficient to find the required asset when the repository contains relatively few of them (in the order of tens).

Textual search. A user should be able to search the catalogue for a string of text contained in any part of the asset description. The result of such a search is zero or more asset descriptions. This function can also take the form of a textual search in the asset body.

Asset retrieval. Given a defined asset (usually found using a search function), a user should be able to retrieve a copy of the asset body.

Organization and search. Browsing is clearly not sufficient to identify the required asset when the repository has a large number of assets, while textual search can be very time consuming. Several techniques can be used in these cases to organize asset descriptions in the catalogue, and thus to facilitate searching. Each technique has an impact on the search and insertion functions. Among these techniques are the following.

- **Keywords.** Each asset is described by one or more keywords (e.g. a C++ linked list could be described by the keywords 'code', 'data structure' and 'C++'). The set of keywords should be defined and managed by the reuse manager. Searching uses one or more keywords as input, and returns zero or more asset descriptions.

- **Faceted classification.** Each asset is described by a set of attribute–value pairs (e.g. the linked list could be described by 'asset type: code', 'asset function: data structure', 'asset implementation language: C++'). Faceted classification is a more rigorous technique than keywords. Searching uses one or more attribute-value pairs as input, and returns zero or more asset descriptions. A more powerful variation of faceted classification defines tree structures for facet values. For instance the attribute 'facet implementation language' could have values 'procedural' or 'object oriented'. The value 'procedural' might be specialized as 'Pascal', 'Fortran' and 'C', and the value 'object oriented' as 'Smalltalk' and 'C++'. Searching can be carried out at any level of the tree. For instance a search on 'implementation language = procedural' returns all assets having values 'Pascal', 'Fortran' or 'C', and a search on 'implementation language = C' restricts the search to assets having value 'C'.

- **Thesaurus.** Each asset is related to other assets by a defined relationship, such as 'is-a', 'similar-to' or 'uses' (e.g. given the 'similar-to' relationship, 'linked list' is similar-to 'double linked-list', 'set' and 'bag'). In this case the searching function takes the form of browsing through assets by following a certain relationship, one asset and one relationship at a time.

History. Each asset description should record author, creation and upgrade dates, and list of modifications. The asset usage should also be traced. For each usage, the context in which the asset has been used and the result (success or failure, ease of use, improvements required, problems met in understanding, testing, integrating and adapting the asset, effort required for those tasks, . . .) should be recorded.

Measurement. The repository tool can automate the collection of data to derive measures (see Chapter 6 for more detail). For instance the tool should collect the number of accesses and retrievals for an asset, the total number of assets, and the number of successful and unsuccessful searches.

Access control. Each of the above functions should be made available to selected roles only. For instance Insertion could be granted to the reuse manager only, Browsing and Retrieval to all users.

Version management. Multiple versions of the same asset should be defined and managed, and their mutual relationships recorded.

Change control. Procedures to require, discuss, accept and implement changes to assets should be defined and enforced by automatic support.

Change notification. Changes to assets (modifications of existing assets, additions and deletions) and to the reuse repository itself (new or modified functions and procedures) should be notified, with automatic support, to all potential users.

We can review these functions in some typical scenarios.

1. A user searches for an asset. The user browses the catalogue, looking at a few asset descriptions, and then searches the catalogue with one keyword.

Too many asset descriptions are returned. The user searches with two keywords. A few asset descriptions are returned. The user browses, finds an interesting asset and retrieves it.

2 A developer reuses an asset. Having searched for an asset, retrieved it, and reused it, a developer or member of a support team updates the asset's history, and requests corrections or improvements.

3. An asset is changed. The reuse manager receives a new, improved version of an asset body developed by the asset owner and decides to integrate the change. The reuse manager notifies all potential users of the change. Reusers can decide to substitute the new asset for the old one in the applications where it has been reused. Another, more restrictive, change policy obliges reusers to substitute the new one. This policy simplifies the management of assets, as only the latest version is stored in the repository.

4. The reuse manager inserts a new asset. A new reusable C++ class is submitted to the reuse manager by a developer. The reuse manager judges the class is potentially reusable, and starts the qualification process (test, code inspection and static code measurement). If the qualification is successful, the reuse manager agrees with the developer on a description for the class, packages it as an asset, inserts the asset in the repository, and notifies all users (or a subset of potentially interested users) that a new class has been inserted.

3.2.3 Non-Functional Requirements

Let's now examine non-functional requirements for the repository.

One or Many Repositories

The repository could be unique, or could be a collection of repositories. The former solution is perfectly suited for small companies; the latter could be considered for large, geographically distributed companies or corporations organized in departments or business units. In that case, assets may be shared at department or business unit level.

With a business unit approach, assets could be traded among units. With a conventional department approach, assets residing in various repositories are available to any department. In both cases a company-wide catalogue of assets should be defined, both to avoid duplications and to disseminate the existence of assets as widely as possible.

Experience Note

Thomson CSF is a large company, with many sites. It is organized in divisions, which behave as independent business units, but are coordinated at company level. The reuse introduction process, the reuse consulting group and reuse techniques are common at company level. The reuse consulting group decided that, given the diversity of businesses among divisions, and given that they are independent profit centers, each of them should have its own repository. No company-wide catalogue exists. However, the reuse repository is always implemented using the company-wide configuration management tool.

All other companies in the SURPRISE experience base are SMEs or independent profit centres not related to large corporations. In all these cases the repository is unique, as clearly there is no necessity for multiple repositories.

Access from Network

As most companies are migrating to a network-centric computing model, a typical requirement is that the repository is seamlessly accessible by any node in a network. For this purpose, a client-server three-tier or N-tier model could be used to implement the repository. With a three-tier model, one layer is dedicated to the storage of elements composing the assets (a file system, database or configuration management system could be used), one layer is dedicated to the packaging of elements into assets, and one layer is dedicated to accessing assets from the network (a web browser or a traditional client application could be used here).

Storage and Production of Asset Bodies

The hard point in choosing or building a repository is solving its interaction with other tools used to produce and possibly store work products that make up the body of assets. A more detailed list of such tool categories is provided later in this Chapter. The common case is interaction with configuration management systems. Such tools give rise to an important non-functional requirement for the reuse repository, as close interaction with them is required.

3.3 Repositories on the Internet

You can access a public repository at http://www.asset.com. This repository contains around 1,000 assets, of various types (code, specifications, reports, training courses . . .) that are available free or on commercial conditions.

Identification and description of assets is made through a standard set of attributes (see Table 3.1). One of the attributes is a list of keywords. Moreover assets are grouped into domains and collections; the same asset can appear in more than one of them. The catalogue is public and accessible through a web browser. Search is by domain, collection, keyword or any attribute value. Retrieval of the asset body is made by file transfer with the FTP protocol. Browsing is public; retrieval is granted if the asset is public, or if its retail price has been paid. The number of hits and downloads is measured.

Table 3.1 Description of an asset in the repository www.asset.com.

Unique Identifier	ASSET_A_766
Asset Name	C++ SOCKET LIBRARY (SOCKET++)
Version	1.7
Release Date	21-MAY-94
Author Name(s)	Gnanasekaran Swaminathan
DETAILS	
Asset Size	55 Files, 987 Kbytes
Computer Environment(s)	IBM RS6000, SUN 4
Computer Language(s)	C++
Distribution	Unlimited
Evaluation Level	ASSET LEVEL 1
Format(s)	C++ Class Library
National Language	English
Supply Date	22-NOV-94
CLASSIFICATION	
Asset Type	SOFTWARE – COMPONENT
Collection	FREEWARE
Domain	NETWORK
	COMMUNICATIONS
	C++ PROGRAMMING
Function	SUPPORTS
Object	NETWORK
Keywords	C++ PROGRAMMING
	IOSTREAM
	SOCKETS

Qualification is provided at four levels, from a simple check that the asset is fairly documented and used, to a full formal independent verification and validation.

We used www.asset.com as an example of a repository of assets. It is only one of a number of sites on the Internet that exist to trade software. A non-exhaustive list comprises www.componentsource.com, www.gamelan.com, www.developer.com and www.software.net. They differ in technical details such as searching method (keywords, programming language, business domain) and area of specialisation (ActiveX components for compo-nentsource.com, Java components for gamelan.com, applications for software.net). What they have in common is that they are working, effective examples of electronic commerce that are changing the way in which soft-ware is developed. On the supplier side, they offer the possibility to any company, anywhere in the world, of delegating distribution, advertising and selling of their products worldwide. On the buyer side they make it possible to choose among a range of existing products at reduced prices, and get them in minutes.

3.4 Tool Categories on the Market

The functions listed in Section 3.2 are common to several software engi-neering tools, so tools not specifically intended to support reuse repositories may provide some of them. In this Section we list such tools, grouped by categories. While specific tools appear and disappear continually on the market, categories are more stable. The aim of this Section is therefore to present the categories which a potential buyer should consider, rather than specific tools. The aim of the Section is not to present an exhaustive list of tools.

Table 3.2 shows the categories vs the functions listed in Section 3.2. The meaning of a Y/N is that the category *typically* does or does not satisfy the function. Therefore specific tools within a category could have a different value from that of the category as a whole.

We now discuss each of the tool categories in Table 3.2.

3.4.1 Reuse-Specific

Reuse-specific tools (such as WEB reuser from Hitachi, Component Manager from Select Software, Object-Catalog from ObjectSpace and SALMS from Sodalia) are usually built on a file system, used to store asset bodies. They package the work products composing an asset body, provide a catalogue of

Table 3.2 Categories of tools and repository functions supported.

REPOSITORY FUNCTIONS	CATEGORIES OF TOOLS Non-reuse repositories				
	Reuse specific tools	Configuration management systems	Repositories for CASE tool integratin	Upper and lower CASE tools	Intranet Groupware tools
Identification and description	Y	Y	Y	Y	N
Insertion	Y	Y	Y	N	Y
Browsing	Y	N	Y	Y	Y
Retrieval	Y	Y	Y	Y	Y
Organization and search	Y	N	N	Y	Y
History	Y	N	N	N	N
Measurement	Y	N	N	N	N
Access control	Y	Y	N	Y	Y
Version management	N	Y	N	N	N
Change control	N	Y	N	N	N
Change notification	Y	N	N	N	Y

asset descriptions, and provide functions to search, browse and retrieve assets. Most of them are simple Windows-like browsers that allow the management of a specific kind of asset (C++ classes, UML models . . .). The most recent ones, such as SALMS, can interface with a data base and a configuration management system (CMS). The database contains the descriptions of assets, while the CMS actually contains the files.

Tools in this category are typically superior to the others as regards asset description, organization and search, and the measurement of access to and use of assets. However, they are reuse-specific and must be well integrated with traditional development tools.

Experience Note

Sodalia developed its own tool called SALMS (Sodalia Asset Library Management System) to manage and give access to a corporate asset repository. It is a three-tier client-server architecture developed in C++. The tool stores asset descriptions in a DBMS and is interfaced with file systems or a CMS (ClearCase) to store the asset bodies. Asset manipulation (insertion, deletion, updates) must be done through SALMS in order to maintain consistency between assets and their descriptions.

SALMS implements most functions described in Section 3.2. Two hundred developers have direct access to the corporate repository, which contains about a hundred large-grained assets (mainly vertical and horizontal libraries, and frameworks of tens or hundreds of classes each). A given asset contains a complete set of work products: requirements and design documents, code, documentation, and tests.

Developing such a tool demanded a major effort. Beyond the fact that it allows Sodalia to have a unique asset 'market place' with facilities for users and administrators, it greatly facilitates the reuse process; in particular, the amount of asset description information (origin, description, integration and adaptation notes . . .) facilitates decision-making when evaluating an asset for reuse.

Three other companies used Euroware, a reuse tool developed as a result of an Esprit project. In total four companies out of 14 used a specific reuse-oriented tool, whereas the others are using traditional software engineering tools (CASE tools, configuration management tools) or no tool at all.

3.4.2 Repositories

Non-reuse repositories can be of three sub-categories. Configuration management systems (with tools such as ClearCase, Continuum, PVCS, Visual Source Safe), repositories to integrate CASE tools on a specific platform (Allegris from Intersolv, Enabler from Softlab, MS-Repository from Microsoft), repositories dedicated to Upper CASE (Rational Rose, Select /OMT, Paradigm Plus . . .) and lower CASE tools (Visual C++, Borland C++, PowerBuilder, Delphi, Visual Basic, NatStar . . .).

CMS tools define a place where work products at the project level are stored, so that project members can access them on a disciplined basis. CMS tools are usually raw environments, without any functions to define asset descriptions or to organize and search for them. Moreover, they are usually oriented to managing fine-grained elements on a project basis, while reusable assets can be large-grained, containing composite elements and of a cross-project nature both in space and time. Of course CMS tools are very suitable as regards access control, change control and version management.

Some missing functions could be defined using the API of the tool, given it exists and it is open. This option should be considered if a company/department has a CMS in place, and no interface is available to a reuse repository.

> ## Experience Note
>
> Eliop, a Spanish company, is using a DBMS to store asset descriptions, and a CMS for storing asset bodies. This resulted in the time-consuming task of keeping them aligned, but did not result in a failure factor because of the limited number of assets. Three other companies, not having a CMS in place, used a DBMS to store asset descriptions, and the file system for storing asset bodies.
>
> Another company had in place a CMS with a user-friendly API. This allowed them to develop an HTML interface for reusable assets stored in their standard CMS. This resulted in an economical and useful solution.

Repositories to integrate CASE tools store files that have to be exchanged among tools. For this purpose they define common protocols and formats for data exchange, and they offer APIs to interface the CASE tools. Compared to CMSs, they take into account the structure (objects, relationships, attributes, . . .) of the elements they are managing. The availability of APIs makes it possible to consider them as an option when they already exist in a company.

Upper and Lower CASE tools need to store and manage files. Some use the file system, some are interfaced with the two sub-categories of repositories listed above. They are the natural place where a user would expect to find functions dealing with asset types such as analysis, design and code. Some of them have built-in functions to deal with reusable items offered by the vendor with the tool (e.g. libraries of classes for data structures and search/sort algorithms), but usually they are not suitable for sharing data at department or company level, since they do not include functions for organizing and searching for assets, and are limited to a project point of view. Since users are very familiar with them, however, they could be considered as an option if they offer an API to extend them, and if the organization defines only assets of the type that they manage.

3.4.3 Intranet and Groupware Tools

Protocols (http, ftp, pop . . .) and technology (web, ftp, wais and email servers, web browsers . . .) going under the umbrella term of the Internet offer a powerful, cheap and open infrastructure that can become the backbone of a reuse repository. Moreover specialized web servers tend to include more and more functions for access control, version management, change control, and interfacing with databases and file systems.

All Internet/Intranet-based solutions share the use of a web browser (such as MS Internet Explorer, or Netscape's Communicator) on the client side to access the catalogue and to download/upload assets. On the server side a web server is needed to publish the catalogue and interface the repository of asset bodies. Basically, the web server can be built in two ways.

- Using and possibly adapting a web server (such as Lotus Domino, Netscape Enterprise Server, etc.). The column Intranet/Groupware tools of Table 3.2 refers to this option.

- Adding a web interface to an existing tool, typically a configuration management system.

Experience Note

Two companies, already using Lotus Notes extensively, defined the reuse repository as a Lotus Notes server, to be accessed by a Lotus Notes client. Six companies built reuse repositories with a web interface, to be accessed on their Intranet by a standard browser. This represents the clearest trend in the SURPRISE experience base.

3.5 Key Points in the Choice of an Asset Repository

The key points in choosing a repository tool are the number of assets that will be stored, the nature of those assets, and the existence and use in the company of other repositories, such as CMS and CASE tools.

If a repository exists, installing another repository for assets duplicates some information, with problems in the long term for maintaining this information and its coherence in the two repositories. The problem can be avoided in two ways. One is extending the non-reuse repository with reuse functions. The other is selecting a reuse repository that interfaces with the non-reuse repository, so that redundant information is synchronized automatically. The practicability of the two options depends on the actual tools available.

The number of assets impacts the difficulty of organizing and searching for assets. The lower their number, the easier it is to build simple search and organization functions on top of tools existing in the company. The higher their number, the greater is the need to use specialized reuse repositories.

Experience Note

Most of the companies and projects in the SURPRISE experience base have a limited number of assets in their repository (below 100), with a majority of fine-grained assets implemented by a single file. The experience has shown that, at this level, how the repository is implemented is not a strategic factor for success. Given that the potential asset reuser is not discouraged from browsing the repository by difficulties in accessing it, nearly any tool and organization of assets is suitable.

Companies took the following options.

- Use a specific reuse tool (4).

- Use the configuration management tool as a reuse repository (3). This option was typically followed by companies having a CMS system in place.

- Use a DBMS to build the catalogue, leaving asset bodies in the file system (3).

- Use and adapt other tools, such as Lotus Domino (2), already available in-house, to build simple catalogues, leaving asset bodies in the file system.

- Use no tools (2).

In a significant number of cases (6) the catalogue was published to be accessed by a web browser.

In general, companies tried to adapt existing tools to serve as reuse repositories, instead of purchasing specific tools. This can be explained partly by cost concerns, but not wholly. Interoperability emerges as the real issue in using or choosing a tool for the repository. Today, the odds are that specific reuse tools are not completely integrated with the other repositories already used by a company (CMS, CASE tools). So companies prefer to undergo the burden of adapting their repositories to offer reuse-specific functions, instead of purchasing (yet another) repository, even if it is better adapted.

In short the suggestion for a company starting a reuse program is as follows:

- if a repository is already in place (CMS or other) try to develop an interface to it offering reuse-specific functions;

- if no repository is in place, develop a simple catalogue of assets with tools already available in the company (DBMS and web server, or files and web server).

One year later or more, when reuse processes are in place and the number of assets starts growing, both in number and granularity, the purchase of a specific reuse repository can be envisaged.

Reuse Processes

4

ABSTRACT

How should reuse be practised, introduced and improved? The aim of this Chapter is to present reuse processes, and to understand why they are necessary, how they relate to traditional software processes, and how they are defined and implemented in the field.

4.1 What Processes Do We Need?

4.1.1 What Is a Process?

Definition

A process is a collection of related tasks leading to a product. Processes are nested: they may be broken down into sub-processes until reaching atomic tasks (sometimes called activities, performed uninterruptedly by one person in one place).

Software processes refer to all the tasks necessary to produce and manage software, whereas reuse processes are that subset of tasks necessary for successful software reuse within a company.

'Reusable asset production' is one reuse process example. It may be broken down into several finer processes like 'reusable asset identification', 'reusable asset development' and 'reusable asset validation'. 'Application development' may be seen, not as a pure reuse process, but as a traditional software process that is obviously impacted by reuse (because developing an application from reusable assets is different from developing an application from scratch).

In this Section, we start from the need: let us analyse what processes are necessary for reuse to be performed efficiently.

4.1.2 Why Are Reuse Processes Necessary?

Processes are necessary to define how an IT department is supposed to perform its activities, and how people work and interact. In particular, defining processes is necessary to ensure efficiency, reproducibility and homogeneity (similar activities are performed in the same way by different company teams at different times).

Adopting new software processes and customizing existing ones are sine qua non conditions for success in reuse. When embarking on reuse, it would not be wise to expect positive results if development teams are allowed to go on working without changing their processes.

Processes must be established in such a way that all reuse-critical tasks are carried out successfully. It is in particular a question of avoiding the risks identified in Table 4.1. The reuse processes corresponding to each of the risks in Table 4.1 are detailed later in this Chapter.

Experience Note

From the SURPRISE experience base, it appears that an important proportion of software houses that practice reuse mainly focus on repository or asset qualification processes, neglecting asset production and support. This is a typical illustration of risk 1: the repository remains almost empty because projects are not supported and assisted to produce assets.

Risks 4, 5 and 6 are generally managed by defining qualification rules and by standardizing technical architectures. However this initiative is generally limited to the definition of a common development environment as opposed to a technical and functional architecture.

Table 4.1 Justification of reuse processes through risks identification.

Risks	Comments and success factors
1. No assets are produced	The production of reusable assets requires an additional effort to take into account external requirements and the implementation of advanced techniques (domain analysis, design, frameworks . . .). These activities must be differentiated from the normal development of applications. ● Reusable asset production should be identified as a process on its own, different from normal production.
2. Assets exist but are not found	Assets must be classified and managed in a centralized way in order to allow potential reusers to find them. ● A central repository or catalogue is essential if certain conditions related to the number of developers and the number of assets are met (see Chapter 3 on repository for more information).
3. It takes too much time to understand and evaluate the asset	Reusers must easily be able to evaluate assets (from technical and functional points of view), in order to decide whether to reuse them. They must be able, if need be, to get support in doing this: it is not their role to immerse themselves in the internal implementation of assets and to correct or adapt them. ● Assets should be packaged with the information necessary for them to be easily evaluated by reusers (see Chapter 2 on assets). ● Within an organization, support in evaluating assets should be provided to reusers by asset owners.
4. Assets are not reusable because their quality is too low	Once assets are produced, their quality and reusability must be guaranteed to future reusers (completeness of documentation, reliability, compliance to company standards . . .). ● A qualification process is necessary to ensure the trustworthiness of assets. ● Do not assume that an asset's quality implies its reusability.
5. Assets are not reusable because they do not meet functional requirements	Obviously, assets must be created not to fulfill one particular need, but a set of needs spread over time. ● Functional domains must be scoped; common functional requirements must be anticipated (this is the objective of domain analysis). ● A common functional architecture must be set up.
6. Assets are not reusable because they do not meet technical requirements	Reused assets must be easy to integrate into the technical architecture of a new application. ● Guidelines and standards are needed to ensure a minimum level of consistency. ● It is absolutely necessary to define a technical architecture that is common to all applications of a family.

Table 4.1 continued

Risks	Comments and success factors
7. The company may not be ready for reuse, or reuse may not be appropriate for its business	Before starting, the company must determine if there is a sufficient potential for reuse and, if yes, how reuse is going to be practised. • A progressive reuse introduction process must be applied.
8. The company is not able to determine if reuse is going in the right direction or if it is profitable	At a corporate or department level, it is difficult to determine how reuse actually improves the business. • Reuse processes, costs and benefits must be monitored in order to achieve continuous assessment and improvement of reuse investment-worthiness. A reuse management process must be set up.
9. Reuse requires new processes and the application of advanced techniques and methods (object design, domain analysis, framework and components . . .)	Project teams must be assisted in these new and specific activities. • A central infrastructure is necessary to coordinate projects, to provide support, and to manage common reusable assets. A reuse support process is essential.

4.1.3 Extending Reuse Boundaries

Chapter 1, Section 1.2, presented the differences between systematic reuse and ad hoc reuse. Obviously, every software developer traditionally reuses existing pieces of software. So why is reuse presented as a key challenge? The point is that the amount of reuse traditionally achieved is generally very small compared to the huge unexploited reuse potential in most IT organizations. There are several reasons for this fact.

- Reuse is often restricted to horizontal reuse in specific technical domains, such as GUI or middleware.

- Existing assets are reused occasionally, when a team member is, by chance, aware of their existence. In this case, the asset originator is generally directly linked (geographically or organizationally) to the reuser; they may even be the same person.

- Reuse often consists merely of picking up existing source code, adapting it if necessary, and incorporating it into another system.

These kinds of practices are generally referred to as ad hoc reuse. Defined and established processes are essential to avoid the pitfalls summarized in the table and to enhance reuse practices. Systematic reuse should take into account the following guidelines.

Reuse should be extended to the whole software lifecycle. It is generally accepted that coding represents no more than 25 per cent (often much less than this figure) of the cost of system development. Thus initiating reuse in the upstream phases generates leverage: reusing requirements assets will probably allow the reuse of subsequent downstream products (design model, code, test cases, documentation . . .). Moreover, if the reuse asset is unchanged, common maintenance will be possible, extending the benefit further.

Reuse should be extended throughout the organization. Assets are part of the capital of the whole organization, and they should be shared through large teams, departments, even perhaps at corporate level. Thus, an asset may be reused even if the producer and consumer are not directly in touch.

Reuse should be extended to multiple domains. Though horizontal reuse of assets in technical domains can often be straightforwardly achieved, vertical reuse of assets in applications domains represents a higher value added for a company. Reuse practices should be progressively spread to any domain for which opportunities have been identified.

Experience Note

Almost all companies we have met are aware of the first of these three recommendations: their assets are rarely limited to code, and include requirements, design and sometimes test cases. Regarding the second and third recommendations, companies that have recently started their reuse programme (the most common case) logically focus on a single business domain and on a restricted team within the organization (one or two pilot projects). More advanced companies have already applied the second and third recommendations.

Thomson, a worldwide corporation, progressively apply reuse to new business domains corresponding to new business units, for which a potential is assessed: air traffic control, training simulators, software engineering tools.

Sodalia, a 300-strong telecommunications software company, has already extended systematic reuse practises to all projects, all software staff and all business domains.

4.1.4 The Producer–Consumer Paradigm

Software providers and IT departments are responsible for providing and maintaining software. Within these activities software development can be regarded as a 'monolithic' set of tasks. Software reuse introduces a differentiation between the tasks related to the production of reusable assets and the tasks related to the production of end-user applications, using those assets as much as possible. The previously monolithic software production process is now split into two families of tasks. These two sets of activities have fundamental differences, but also similarities. It is interesting to compare them since it is one way of characterizing reuse processes (see Table 4.2).

Table 4.2 Comparison of application production and reusable asset production.

Applications	Reusable assets
Consumers	
The 'consumer' is the end user.	The 'consumer' is the application developer.
Products	
The product is an application or system for the end user.	The product is a software asset that is ready to be integrated in several applications.
Product 'marketing'	
On the external market, or internally within the business.	Internally, within the IT department
Product documentation	
Application end user guide. Design and maintenance documentation.	Asset user guide. Asset reference manual. Asset design documentation.
Customer support	
End user support, given by support team.	Asset user support, given by asset owner or reuse support group.
Product management and maintenance	
Application operation. Application maintenance.	Asset management. Asset maintenance.
Development technologies	
Traditional development technologies	More 'advanced technologies' like object oriented frameworks and component-based architecture may be needed.
Development methods	
Traditional software engineering methods	Domain analysis, domain engineering, framework development.
Validation	
Validation according to end users' requirements.	Validation according to domain definition, company strategy, guidelines . . .

These differences and similarities are summarized in *Fig. 4.1.*

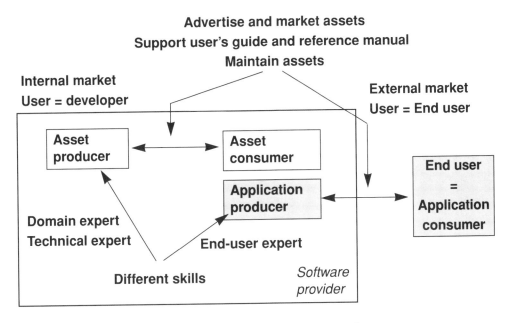

Fig. 4.1 The producer – consumer paradigm.

Note that whereas the above-mentioned theoretical comparison always applies, some companies have chosen not to organize themselves following the producer–consumer paradigm. For instance, Chase Computer Services, which has a small software organization (less than 30 people), has chosen not to specialize software developers. All of them have at the same time the role of asset producer and application producer. See Chapter 9 on experiences for more information.

4.1.5 Different Ways of Practising Reuse

How is reuse practised and, in particular, how does it affect traditional software processes? This question may have several answers according to the degree of commitment of the company to reuse. Three possible solutions are summarized in Table 4.3.

Table 4.3 Risks and benefits associated with reuse practices.

Characterization of reuse	Software processes	Benefits ("B.") and Risks ("R.")
Integrated to projects	Traditional software processes (like application development) are mixed with reuse processes (like asset production, asset usage). Projects produce applications and reusable assets at the same time following the same processes.	B. Few organizational changes. R. Difficulty of avoiding short-term pressure for project completion. R. Development techniques for applications and reusable assets are not differentiated.
Anticipated	Focus on production of reusable assets. They are developed independently from applications, with different techniques, possibly by different teams.	B. Roles are distinguished. B. Skills are partitioned. R. Requires coordination with projects.
A posteriori	Focus on re-engineering. Applications are developed without reuse in mind. Potential reusable assets are identified and extracted afterwards.	B. Does not disrupt application development projects. R. Assets are not initially designed for reuse. R. Possible lack of efficiency (effort overhead trying to package what was not initially intended to be reusable).

Another important distinction between ways of practising reuse resides in the difference between black box and white box reuse that has been introduced in Chapter 1. This distinction applies not only to the assets themselves, but also to the reuse process. For instance, in the case of black box reuse, the asset usage process and the asset maintenance process are impacted by the fact that assets cannot be modified when reused.

Experience Note

From the SURPRISE experience base, we observe that very few companies are performing black box reuse, and none has selected exclusively this option. Several explanations are possible:

● white box reuse is easier and less demanding in term of expertise and design effort;

● white box reuse is more flexible: it gives more freedom to the reuser;

- allowing white box reuse makes the number of reuse assets increase;

- some practitioners argue that, by nature, an asset must be adapted to the context in which it is reused.

4.1.6 An Overview of Reuse Processes

At this stage, we have identified what kinds of processes are needed and why, we have defined different ways of practising reuse, and we have characterized reuse processes within software processes. Basically, we have identified the need for five main reuse processes.

Asset production: asset identification, development and classification.

Asset usage: locating and evaluating assets, and achieving their actual reuse by integrating them into applications being developed. This is the part of the traditional application development process that is impacted by reuse.

Asset management: asset storage, repository management (if any), and asset dissemination (through a database or a catalogue).

Maintenance and support: support for asset usage (to reusers), methodological support (to asset developers and reusers), and corrective and evolutionary maintenance of assets.

Reuse management: introducing and monitoring reuse within a company or department. This includes tracking reuse results, coordinating reuse activities, and defining and improving reuse processes. It is in particular important to define how reuse will impact existing software processes (see Section 4.4) and to define the process for developing an application from existing assets.

These processes, with their underlying sub-processes, are summarized in *Fig. 4.2*.

Each box represents a reuse-specific process that needs to be defined in order to minimize risks. These processes may have different granularities: some are simple and atomic (asset extraction ...) others may be very complex (domain analysis).

In the earlier Section entitled 'Why are reuse processes necessary?', the risks table (Table 4.1) shows that not considering these processes as a whole is a critical risk for the success of the reuse programme.

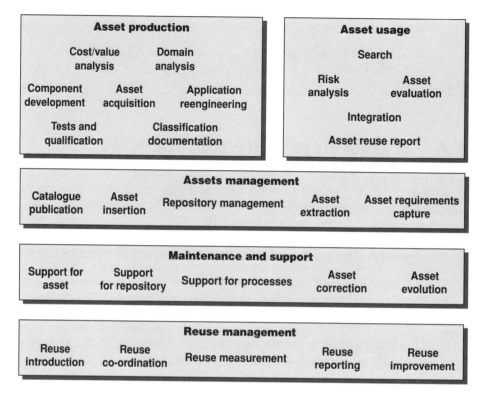

Fig. 4.2 Main reuse processes.

4.1.7 Who Does What?

Once these processes have been defined, responsibilities must be assigned in order to ensure that they will be carried out and monitored correctly. Roles must be defined and assigned to one or several individuals in the current organization. Here is a non-exhaustive list of the main roles involved in reuse.

Definition

REUSE-SPECIFIC ROLES

- **Reuse Manager:** responsible for monitoring the overall reuse programme.

- **Asset Library Manager:** manages asset storage and configuration, and ensures assets are accessible to developers.

- **Reuse Support Member:** supports projects in applying reuse processes and methods.

- **Asset Owner:** maintains assets.

- **Asset Producer:** creates assets.

- **Asset Reuser:** actually reuses existing assets.

TRADITIONAL ROLES IMPACTED BY REUSE

- **Project Manager:** has to take reuse objectives into account and possibly has to coordinate with other projects.

- **Software Architect:** must ensure architecture facilitates asset reuse.

- **Software Engineer:** must be involved in the reuse programme.

- **Analyst / Domain Expert:** helps to produce domain models and to qualify vertical assets.

Each of these roles must be clearly assigned to a person or a group of people.

We have now defined the requirements in term of processes for a company. Let's now examine some of the processes identified above. Section 4.2 discusses reuse introduction (part of the reuse management process). Section 4.3 deals with actual reuse practice (asset production and usage, as well as maintenance and support processes). In both Sections, some well recognized reuse process models are presented, together with some examples of how they have been applied (or not applied!) in the field.

Other processes are detailed in other Chapters. Asset management is described in Chapter 2 (reusable software assets), and Chapter 3 (reuse repository) and reuse management is dealt with in Chapter 1 (introducing software reuse) and Chapter 5 (managing reuse).

4.2 Starting a Corporate Reuse Programme: The Reuse Introduction Process

How to start? There are so many issues to be addressed when starting reuse that one must be careful to do things in the right order!

The following questions should be asked and answered, in the sequence shown.

- What are my business objectives? How will reuse contribute to them?
- Given those objectives, is reuse the right solution? Is there a strong potential for reuse in the domain(s) in which my company develops software?
- Is my company ready to start reuse? Is it sufficiently mature, or are other improvement actions necessary prior to reuse?
- What are the risks? Why might reuse fail?
- What actions should I undertake to minimize those risks?
- Have those actions been successful?

Those questions should be answered in the light of key factors such as company strategy, management, organization, human aspects, development process, architecture and technologies.

Experience Note

The analysis of how reuse has been introduced in the companies represented in the SURPRISE experience base reveals that the problem is rarely addressed as a whole. Companies too often restrict their investigations to the identification of potential benefits that are not clearly related to business goals. Expected benefits generally concern software production (productivity, quality).

Few companies have a clear business vision of what reuse will bring them. In particular, companies do not define the scope of the reuse programme and its priority in term of business goals. They do not relate software reuse to market requirements. They seldom deeply analyse the potential of their businesses concerning software reuse. Implementing a reuse programme is too often a software decision instead of a business decision.

4.2.1 Should I Go for Reuse?

Reuse is not an all-purpose solution. Reuse will not automatically bring productivity and quality improvement to any company in any situation. This Section provides a decision grid (Table 4.4) to determine if it is really appropriate to introduce reuse.

Table 4.4 Reuse introduction decision grid.

Criteria to be considered	Questions to be answered
Market position	• Do I need to improve my software process? • Do I need to improve the efficiency of my business IS? • What is my position in the market? • What are my competitors doing? • Do I need to invest to improve my efficiency and my competitiveness? Investing in reuse is justified if the company needs to reinforce its position in the market.
Business opportunities	• Is the activity of my company/department well structured into business domains with recurring applications/systems in each domain? • Is software a critical issue for the success of my business? Investing in reuse may not be worthwhile if the company does not have a software-intensive business and if the activity is not structured into applications families or product lines.
Company strategy	• Do I need to improve my business reactivity? • Do I need to build product lines? • Do I need to capitalize knowledge of business domains? • Do I need to improve the efficiency of my IS? There are three main reasons to introduce reuse: • to capitalize on business domains; • to build product lines or reinforce the company offer; • to improve IS and its consistency with the business.
SOFTWARE DEVELOPMENT	
Functional stability	• Are my functional requirements stable with identified variabilities? If not, the scope of software reuse may be limited to technical and generic assets.
Technical stability	• Are my software development environments, tools and platforms well defined and stable? If not, the company should first focus on domain models and business objects.
Process maturity	• Does the company have an acceptable maturity level regarding software engineering? • Has it adopted a quality system, an agreed software life-cycle, architecture, best practices . . .? If not, it may be too early to implement a reuse programme right now. But it may not be too early to think about it: reuse must be anticipated.

Table 4.4 continued

Criteria to be considered	Questions to be answered
STAFF Technology mastery	• Are the development teams well experienced in development technologies? Mastery of implementation technologies and design techniques may be seen as a prerequisite to putting reuse into practice.
Motivation and change acceptance	• Is the staff ready to accept changes? • What should be done to ensure motivation? Reuse will never be institutionalized without a clear answer to these questions.

4.2.2 The Software Productivity Consortium Reuse Adoption Process

Experience Note

Thomson, a French systems engineering corporation, has applied the Reuse Adoption Process to drive reuse introduction in several different business units dealing with different domains. Reuse has been introduced into different engineering domains: air traffic control, supervision and control, software engineering tools, and training simulation systems. In every case, the introduction process comprised the following steps:

● definition of reuse objectives;

● understanding the business context by performing (a) a domain assessment to evaluate reuse potential and (b) a reuse capability assessment to evaluate if the department is ready for reuse;

● risk analysis and reuse strategy definition;

● definition of an action plan to start reuse or to improve reuse practices;

● implementation of the action plan and review.

This reuse introduction process has been coordinated by a reuse team, common to the whole corporation. Other domains such as air defence systems and train traffic control have been assessed, but have appeared to offer a lower potential for reuse. The main advantage of this approach is that it is business oriented. It is an iterative approach, applied periodically in order to drive not only reuse introduction but also reuse improvement.

The Software Productivity Consortium (SPC)[1] has developed a Reuse Adoption Process. It defines several activities necessary to introduce and improve reuse practices. It also provides managers with decision taking support. After having introduced reuse inside the company, let us now examine how reuse should be practised.

4.3 Practising Reuse: Asset Production and Application Production Processes

4.3.1 The REBOOT Process Model

REBOOT (Karlsson, 1995)[2] is a European ESPRIT project that played a key role in defining reuse processes. This model mainly focuses on the producer-consumer chain. As in a traditional V model (where there is a mapping from production steps to validation steps), there is a correspondence between the steps of producing and consuming reusable assets:

- assets are developed by project X in order to be reused by project Y;

- assets are qualified by project X in order to be evaluated by project Y;

- assets are classified and inserted in a repository by project X in order to be retrieved and extracted from the repository by project Y.

Separate projects are responsible for performing development *for* reuse (i.e. produce, qualify and classify reusable assets) and development *with* reuse (i.e. search for, evaluate and integrate existing assets to build systems). This model is nice because it is easy to understand, and introduces a symmetry between production and consumption. Its main drawback is that it may be interpreted as being too project-centric, and it is fitted to small-grained components rather than to product lines or business information systems.

Experience Note

REBOOT processes have been successfully applied in the domains of embedded and control systems, mainly in the telecommunications and industrial fields. For instance an Italian systems engineering company has launched an internal reuse programme. They adapt their traditional cascade system engineering lifecycle to reuse by introducing development *with* reuse (identification of existing assets to be reused during requirements analysis and preliminary design) and development *for* reuse (identification of reusable assets to be developed at the preliminary design stage and extraction of reusable assets once the system has been developed: post-development analysis).

4.3.2 Jacobson, Griss and Jonsson Process Model

In their book entitled *Software Reuse* (Jacobson, 1997)[3], the authors have defined three main development processes.

Application Family Engineering consists in designing and implementing a functional architecture fitted to a family of applications or a product line. This common and stable architecture will be the starting point for developing applications and assets.

Component System Engineering consists in developing reusable components (or assets) by analysing requirements and their variability through the different applications of a family.

Application System Engineering is the process of building applications based on the common architecture and using existing assets.

This approach provides a broad and clear modelling process for reuse. It is very well fitted to product lines. However, in the case of business IS, we also often have application families (for instance financial product management applications are families of applications where financial products can vary) and domain models.

This approach is very close to what is generally called domain engineering (as opposed to application engineering). We can consider that the first two processes (AFE and CSE) constitute domain engineering activities.

Experience Note

We only found one example of such an advanced approach, and it was based on modelling in UML (Unified Modelling Language). Sodalia, an Italian telecommunications software company, is applying domain engineering to develop object oriented vertical (i.e. application-specific) frameworks. This case is described in the next Section, on domain engineering.

4.3.3 Should I Practise Domain Engineering?

Domain engineering consists of defining architecture, analysing requirements and developing software, not for a single application but for a family of applications (existing, to be developed or potential). It is naturally an activity or a process that leads to reusable assets.

Domain analysis is a part of the domain engineering process. Domain analysis was first introduced by Jim Neighbors in 1980 as 'the activity of identifying objects and operations of a class of similar systems in a particular domain'. Since then, various definitions and methodologies (e.g. SEI's FODA: Feature Oriented Domain Analysis) have been proposed. Domain analysis aims to maximize reuse within a given domain, by attempting to capture its commonalities and variabilities in a set of software assets. Such an activity requires a good understanding of the domain, and the participation of domain experts together with software engineers.

Domain engineering, and domain analysis in particular, are of great value for companies who have well-defined product lines. They also serve to capture, formalize and exchange domain knowledge. Domain knowledge is a precious company asset, but it is easily lost if it remains simply in the minds of human experts. Domain analysis makes it possible to build real, added-value, business objects which capture domain knowledge.

Application reengineering, when it is done with the objective of reuse (extract assets from existing applications), is often a domain engineering activity: studying existing applications is a way of studying a domain.

Experience Note

Sodalia frequently applies domain engineering to the network management domain. Its domain analysis process is close to Jacobson's Application Family Engineering, and is based on the following activities:

- domain scoping: domain boundaries and terminology definition;

- domain requirements, with Use Case;

- domain modelling, using UML notation;

- domain architecture design.

Commonality and variability across known (past or future) 'instantiations' of the application are quantitatively analysed.

This domain analysis activity naturally leads to asset development (equivalent to Jacobson's Component System Engineering). In the case of this company, the domain analysis is used to build object oriented business frameworks (in C++ and using distribution models like CORBA: see Chapter 7 for more information on these aspects). Such frameworks are specific to telecommunications network management. In its first year, a framework is instantiated three or four times. Frameworks are well fitted to domain analysis implementation because, by definition, they include the notion of commonality and variability.

Figure 4.3. illustrates the process just described.

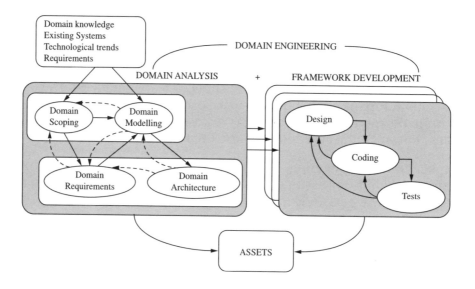

Fig. 4.3 Sodalia's domain engineering process.

Such approaches may be considered as very advanced and efficient ways to achieve reuse. However, it is not free of risk: domain engineering is a time-consuming activity, requiring both advanced modelling skills and domain expertise.

To summarize, we can identify the following success factors.

- Domain engineering is the most efficient way to practise vertical reuse and to develop business objects.

- Before starting, domain potential must be assessed and domain boundaries must be clearly defined.

- Software analysts must work together with domain experts (to obtain input information and validate models) and with application developers (to use domain models as the basis for application modelling).

4.3.4 Processes in the Field

Processes are abstract, and for most companies it is generally difficult to draw a clear vision of their processes from their current practices. There is a gap between theoretical process models and actual practices. That is mainly because processes are not always rigorously defined and/or applied.

Software process maturity has appeared to be a very important reuse facilitator. Many reuse failure cases can be explained by the fact that reuse processes were based on software processes that were not sufficiently stable and reproducible prior to reuse introduction.

- Reuse requires a strong software process.

- Testing and quality processes must be adapted to reusable assets.

- The configuration management process must include assets as a new type of software product.

- The maintenance process must include asset maintenance and its impact on applications maintenance.

Reuse should be thought of early (for instance when starting the migration to a new generation of technologies), but its introduction normally should not happen until other software processes have reached a sufficient level of maturity.

Experience Note

Companies generally define a repository management process and a process to validate or qualify reusable assets. Too often, reuse processes are limited to these aspects. Repository management is sometime linked with the company configuration management policy. In other cases, reusable assets are managed separately.

Domain analysis is far from being systematically applied, even in fields where there is a potential for it. Asset development is very rarely differentiated from application development: very few companies practising reuse have a specific process to identify reusable asset requirements and to produce the corresponding assets. Consequently, reusable assets are identified by the team which will also use them for the first time, without necessarily taking other requirements into account: that tends to reduce reusability.

None of the companies we met have a real reuse improvement process, although the two most advanced have a reuse monitoring process.

Sodalia, a company that is very successful in reuse, has formalized and put into practice one of the most complete set of reuse processes, including:

- domain engineering, resulting in framework development;
- development of vertical and horizontal assets;
- external asset acquisition;
- asset qualification (for both internal and external assets);
- asset classification and repository management (asset description, linked with a configuration management system that manages asset content);
- asset maintenance;
- application development process;
- reuse management (organization, monitoring, reporting, training, communication).

4.3.5 Qualifying and Evaluating Assets

As mentioned in Chapter 2, candidate assets should be qualified or evaluated against more than usually demanding criteria (general quality criteria, functional criteria, technical and architectural criteria). This action can be done in two situations, corresponding to two different processes:

- validating an asset before insertion into a common repository, or before officially declaring it as reusable;
- checking that an asset meets one's requirements before reusing it.

Experience Note

In the field, assets are generally qualified according to quality criteria, one of them being the completeness of the associated set of work products. Qualifying an asset is generally limited to checking the existence of the following work products that accompany an asset:

- general information about the asset;
- asset (re)user documentation;
- asset analysis and design models;
- test reports and test cases.

The qualification process is rarely based on metrics calculated on assets.

Usually, companies do not have a formalized evaluation process (before reusing an asset).

Who qualifies assets? Often that is not clearly determined, or is informally done by the asset originator, or is mixed with quality review. Only one company we met distinguishes reusable asset qualification reviews from application quality reviews. In this case, each type of review is led by different people since the reuse group is separate from the quality group. This last example is obviously a good solution since three different objectives are not mixed: quality objectives, reuse objectives and project objectives.

4.3.6 Managing Risks When Reusing

Qualification and evaluation can be seen as risk management activities.

Before Creating an Asset

Developing a reusable asset is an investment. Thus there is a decision-taking process to minimize risks. If the following questions are not answered, the investment of developing the asset may not be profitable.

- Is this asset significant for the business of the company?
- What is the business potential? What is the probability that there will be a similar requirement?

- Who are the potential reusers?

- What is the cost overhead, compared to developing the same software without reusability?

The decision to develop a reusable asset should be taken only after having considered the answers to the above questions.

Before Reusing an Existing Asset

Reusing an asset may also include some risks.

- Is the asset compatible with my architecture constraints?

- Does the asset meets my functional requirements?

- If not, should I adapt the asset or my requirements? In both cases what is the loss or gain in terms of functionality?

- How is my application likely to evolve? Will I, or someone else, be able to make the incorporated asset evolve satisfactorily?

- Are there any property or legal constraints that apply to the reused asset or to the resulting application?

- What is the cost of developing the application (or part of it) without the asset?

- What is the cost of understanding, testing and adapting the asset?

Having answered these questions, one is able to take the right decision based on a comparison of the effort saved against the identified risks.

4.3.7 Advertising Assets

How will someone whose need may be fulfilled by an existing asset know that it exists? Three situations can be found in practice relating to this issue.

- The person will never be aware of the existence of the asset unless (s)he is directly in touch with its originator. This situation corresponds to ad hoc reuse.

- The person knows that, if the asset exists, it can be found in one place, a common repository, classified following a predetermined scheme.

- When a new asset is available, all those potentially interested are notified. This situation corresponds to a 'push' communication strategy (in contrast to the previous one which is 'pull').

86

Ideally, the second and third solutions should be mixed.

Experience Note

In the field, companies are generally in the first or second situation. Lots of them use a faceted classification scheme to retrieve assets: see Chapter 3 (reuse repository) for more information on faceted classification.

4.3.8 Communicating About Reuse

Reuse success requires the involvement and motivation of the whole software staff. This objective can't be reached without a good level of communication. Several forms of communication can be envisaged.

- Periodically report reuse results (in terms of produced assets, reused assets, efficiency . . .) to management.

- Organize communication events where reuse intermediate results, improvement strategy and objectives are presented to software staff.

- Provide news about assets, processes and tools to software staff.

- Establish interest groups to define improvement strategies.

These communications can employ a variety of channels: reports, newsletters, meetings, and intranet or other messaging or groupware systems.

Experience Note

Almost all companies report reuse results to management. Few have implemented other means of communication.

Thomson has set up a Common Efficiency Team in order to share experiences and define improvement strategies at corporate level.

Sodalia periodically organizes communication events to present consolidated reuse results to the staff. Their internal repository also maintains reuse news.

4.3.9 Maintaining Assets

A company involved in reuse has to solve several issues.

Who Should Maintain Assets?

For efficiency reasons, the reuser should not be in charge of corrective and evolutionary maintenance of an asset he is reusing. As for any software product, the asset (re)user must benefit from support and maintenance, and should not have to understand or to modify the internal aspects of the asset. Thus, a person should be identified to play the role of owner (i.e. responsible for maintenance and evolution) of an asset: it could be the asset originator or a member of a reuse support team. In the first case, support should be efficient because the developer knows the asset well, but (s)he may not be sufficiently available for support activities if (s)he is involved in other tasks or projects. In the second case, a knowledge transfer from the asset developer to the asset owner is required.

How Does Maintenance Affect an Asset's Users?

An additional reason to avoid asset evolution or correction being undertaken by asset users is obviously to control the changes. The benefit of reusing common software is partially lost if maintenance is done separately by every reuser. The asset must be changed in a centralized way, under the responsibility of the asset owner. As for a software product, applications that use the asset must be notified of the new version and then have the choice to incorporate the change or not. In some companies the systematic integration of new asset versions into customer applications is made mandatory.

- In any application, reused asset boundaries must be kept clear in order to make separate maintenance of the asset possible.

- Each asset must keep track of its (re)users for maintenance purposes, so as to be able to notify them when the asset is updated.

How To Avoid Conflicts?

The above solution is satisfactory for corrective maintenance. Concerning the functional or technical evolution of assets, conflicts may happen if different users of an asset have incompatible requirements for its evolution. To solve this problem, we can define two guidelines.

- Asset evolution is determined by asset owners in accordance with company strategy and domain evolution. The reuse support group is better qualified to embody this common vision than an application group, which by definition does not have a global vision and is subject to different constraints.

● Incorporating a new asset version into an application that uses this asset should be optional, decided by the application leader, who must in any case be informed of the availability of the new version.

Experience Note

In most cases, evolution of assets is generally left to the reuser, who has no support for doing it. Consolidation of any modification into the original asset is rarely made. Thus assets are duplicated and rapidly diverge. In consequence development teams only obtain a benefit from reuse at development time (and not during maintenance).

4.3.10 Managing and Improving Reuse Efficiency

Like any other activity, reuse must be monitored and controlled. Reuse management must address the following issues: project co-ordination, reporting on reuse, improving reuse strategy and processes, communication (discussed above), staff motivation and training, and reuse organization (definition and adoption of roles regarding reuse).

Experience Note

Companies generally produce periodical reuse reports. This is necessary to have a complete and integrated view of reuse practices within the company and thus to try to improve them. Concerning reuse co-ordination, only one company maintains a 'reuse history' of every asset. Moreover, no company manages requests for asset creation or modification: this would be a way to ease the asset creation decision process by taking into account both developers' needs and business strategy.

More management issues are discussed in Chapter 5 (managing reuse). We have described the main reuse processes. The next Section analyses their impact on traditional software processes.

4.4 A Summarized Vision on Processes: How Does Reuse Affect Traditional Software Processes?

Let us base our discussion on the standard ISO 12207 software process model. Major processes are shown in the following simplified diagram (*Fig. 4.4*).

The observed impact of reuse (McClure, 1997)[4] on traditional software processes (Table 4.5) consists in introducing the distinction between application-related products and reusable assets, and the distinction between the corresponding processes. For instance, some of the above software processes can be split into two variations, corresponding to applications and reusable assets. The two variations have different constraints.

- Application processes are subject to general cost, quality and time-to-market constraints.

- Reusable asset processes are mainly constrained by fitting into company strategy, capturing domain expertise, building product families . . .

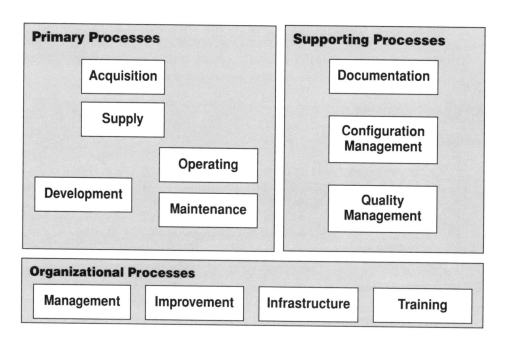

Fig. 4.4 Main traditional software processes.

Table 4.5 Impact of reuse on traditional software processes.

Traditional Software Process (according to ISO 12207)	Variation introduced by reuse practices
Primary processes	
Acquisition	Must include not only turnkey application/system acquisition, but also software asset acquisition (see the Section in Chapter 2 on acquiring software assets).
Supply	This process is mostly unchanged if the final customer is not aware of reuse. Otherwise, reuse may lead to a trade-off between costs and functionality.
Development	This is traditionally an application or system development process. • Each step of this process (analysis, architecture, design . . .) is impacted by reuse: reusable assets must be searched for, evaluated and integrated. • A new 'domain engineering' process must be introduced (domain analysis and vertical reusable asset development are part of it).
Operating	Reuse has no impact on this process.
Maintenance	Application or system maintenance must be differentiated from asset maintenance. This aspect has been discussed above.
Supporting processes	
Documentation	System documentation (both user documentation and engineering documentation) must be differentiated from asset documentation (mainly asset user documentation).
Configuration management	Assets may be managed in the same CM repository as applications, but asset changes should be controlled separately from application changes. In both cases a new asset management process is necessary.
Quality management	The quality system applies both to systems development and asset development. A potential difference is that assets are internal work products, not delivered directly to external customers.
Organizational processes	
Management	Should include reuse scoping, reuse planning, reuse control.
Infrastructure	Should include the management of reuse tools, and in particular the technical infrastructure necessary to give access to and manage an asset repository.
Training	Should include training in reuse, for managers and practitioners.
Improvement	Should include reuse process definition, assessment and

References

1. Software Productivity Consortium, *Reuse Adoption Guidebook,* http://www.software.org
2. Karlsson, E.A. (1995) *Software Reuse, A Holistic Approach.* John Wiley & Sons.
3. Jacobson I., Griss M. and Jonsson P. (1997) *Software Reuse.* Addison Wesley.
4. McClure, C. *Extending the Software Process to Include Reuse.* Symposium on Software Reusability, 1997.

Managing Reuse

5

ABSTRACT

This Chapter discusses three management requirements that are of critical importance to the success of a reuse initiative, and which concern both business managers and software managers. They are: to decide whether the organization should embark on a systematic reuse initiative; to gain maximum commitment to, and involvement in, the reuse initiative; and to decide on the allocation of reuse-related responsibilities.

5.1 The Management Issues

In the spirit of the whole of this book, it is not the purpose of this Chapter to set out recipes for the management of a reuse initiative, or detailed check-lists of management 'do's and 'don't's. Instead, the purpose is to raise some key management issues, in the expectation that the general principles identified can be transferred to the specific circumstances and management styles of readers' own organizations.

Setting aside some of the more routine and mundane management activities – things like budgeting, scheduling or reporting, that can reasonably be taken for granted in any organization – there are five key requirements that confront management with respect to a systematic reuse initiative. They are set out in *Fig. 5.1*.

The fourth and fifth of those requirements, concerning issues of process and measurement, are addressed separately in Chapter 4 (on process) and Chapter 6 (on measurement). The present Chapter addresses the first three issues.

- Decide whether to adopt systematic software reuse as a value-generating element of business strategy.
- Gain maximum commitment to, and involvement in, the reuse initiative.
- Decide on the allocation of reuse-specific responsibilities.
- Integrate reuse with other software processes, and integrate the reuse introduction initiative with other software process improvement initiatives.
- Determine quantified goals for reuse, and establish measurements that management can use to control progress toward achieving those goals.

Fig. 5.1 Key requirements for managing reuse.

5.2 To Reuse or Not To Reuse? – the Big Question

'To be or not to be' is not just a celebrated quotation. It is the central issue on which the drama of Hamlet turns. 'To reuse or not to reuse' is similarly a central issue for organizations caught up in the drama of trying to escape the software crisis. For the management of such organizations, the question may pose as deep a challenge as Hamlet's.

In Chapter 1, we developed the broad proposition that systematic software reuse holds out the promise of radical improvements in productivity, quality and business performance, and that the achievement of those improvements is contingent on the nature of the organization's software portfolio and on the investment of substantial effort. That proposition implies a question (*Fig. 5.2*) that every organization should answer, before committing itself to systematic reuse.

To reuse or not to reuse . . . Just because it is *possible* to make radical improvements, it does not mean that it is the *right* business decision. The long decades of the software crisis are littered with stories of improvements that were attempted just because they were possible, without any analysis of the business case. Even if productivity and quality improve, the effects on

If the nature of the software portfolio means that systematic reuse has the potential to achieve radical improvements in software productivity and quality, will the achievement of those improvements lead in turn to increased value for the business, sufficient to justify the necessary large cost of investing in the change?

Fig. 5.2 The big question!

business performance may constitute an inadequate return on the effort invested; worse, the effects might even be negligible or negative.

In his book *The Process Edge: Creating Value Where It Counts*, Peter Keen (Keen, 1997)[1] calls this 'the process paradox', and characterizes it as 'the startling fact that businesses can decline and even fail at the same time that process reform is dramatically improving efficiency by saving the company time and money and improving product quality and customer service'. He goes on: 'The companies that have suffered from the process paradox – those whose process reform success was met by business stagnation or failure – clearly got some process right. But that is much different from getting the *right* process right.' And: 'Getting the right process right means using capital to build wealth: getting the wrong one right casts the illusion of success but cracks the foundation – or fails to build it. Reduced costs, enhanced service or increased profits translate to value only if they generate a cash flow that exceeds the amount of capital used to achieve those benefits.' Finally: 'The 1990s may well be the period of multi-reengineering chaos, just as the 1980s was the period of multi-technology chaos.'

The general message of Peter Keen's book, exemplified by those extracts, is that process improvement cannot be guaranteed to translate into value for the enterprise. That general message applies to software reuse initiatives just as much as to any other changes in business or software processes. If those extracts whet your appetite, by making you want to understand the underlying arguments, there is no substitute for reading the book. In the meantime, let us try to communicate the simple essentials of Keen's case (*Fig. 5.3*), which should be understood by all those business Hamlets asking the question, 'To reuse or not to reuse?'

According to Fig. 5.3, the challenge for management, when considering whether or not to embark on systematic software reuse, is twofold.

The first challenge is to understand the worth and salience of the software development process for the enterprise. Is it a key business capability, earning more than it costs or, if not, should it be? Can it be used to change the 'rules of the game' for competitors, or to recover a disadvantage created by a competitor who itself has changed the rules of the game?

If the answers are 'yes', the second challenge is to decide whether systematic software reuse is an appropriate way of investing in software process change. Does the organization's software development portfolio offer substantial reuse potential? Will an investment in reuse earn more than it costs? Would some other change in the software process (eg inspections) yield higher net earnings? If reuse appears to be the best available software process investment, how does it compare with investing in other business process improvements?

- Business processes (including software processes) are part of an organization's capital, even though they are not usually recognized as investment or accounted for as such.
- Present proposals for business process change should accordingly be treated as investment decisions, and analysed according to the same standards as other investment decisions. The analysis should focus rigorously on economic value, rather than on the broader (and vaguer) concept of benefits. However much benefits may be quantified and desirable (for instance 50 per cent higher productivity), the real test should be whether they translate into economic value for the business in terms of cash flow. Rigour should also be applied in identifying all the costs of change (training, support, severance, etc.), not just the more obvious up-front ones, in deciding whether the investment in change will yield net added value.
- Processes (as capital) may be classified according to their worth – whether they add value to the business or subtract value from it. Value-adding processes generate value to the business in excess of the costs that they consume: they are assets. Value-subtracting processes, on the other hand, are liabilities: they consume costs in excess of the value they generate to the business. An organization's process strategy should be to maximize the worth of all processes.
- Processes may also be classified according to their salience – the extent to which they are essential to the performance and valuation of the business in the marketplace. Non-essential processes should be candidates for discontinuing, outsourcing, breaking up and part-recombining with other processes, etc. Essential (high-salience) processes should be targeted for improvement to maximize their worth, especially if they represent a real competitive edge.

Fig. 5.3 *The essentials of Keen's 'economic value added' argument.*

The questions can be alternatively looked at in terms of a SWOT analysis (strengths, weaknesses, opportunities, threats), applied first to the business and then to the software process. Do the strengths and weaknesses of the business, and the opportunities and threats facing it, indicate that it has the potential and the readiness (even the imperative need) to gain value from a programme of systematic software reuse? Similarly, do the strengths and weaknesses of the software process, and the opportunities and threats facing it, indicate that it has the potential and the readiness to accommodate the major change represented by a reuse programme, and to integrate it with other (enforced or discretionary) changes?

Answering such questions is rarely easy. Doing it the Peter Keen way involves an understanding of *economic value added (EVA)*, an indicator that is increasingly being adopted by leading companies as 'a sensitive indicator of value creation, a rational tool for financial planning and management decision making, and a fair standard for ownership-like incentives' (Milano, 1997[2]). Beware though: even Peter Keen calls it a 'very complex subject'! He recommends two references (Stewart, 1991[3]; Copeland, 1995[4]).

You may feel you lack the time or inclination to master the technicalities of EVA. At least, however, ask the questions. It is almost certainly better to have intuitive, 'finger in the wind' answers to the *right* questions than to have logically constructed and exactly calculated answers to the *wrong* ones. Asking the questions means that you are placing the reuse issue in the right business context for your organization, and avoiding what might be called 'the Everest syndrome' – attempting to climb the mountain *just because it's there*, just because it sets a challenge and offers all kinds of feel-good benefits to reward success.

The mountain is too big and dangerous, and the costs of equipping the expedition are too high, to undertake the climb for inadequate reasons. 'No pain, no gain', the saying goes. The trouble is that just suffering pain does not itself guarantee any gain. Introducing reuse, like climbing Everest, cannot be done without pain; so let's be sure about the gains to be found on the route to the summit.

The purpose of this book, however, is to encourage, not to discourage. The preceding paragraph is just a warning against the kind of bravado that may lead to failure. If you set yourself to find answers to the questions above, and if you end up with a confident and reasonably well founded belief that systematic software reuse can add value to your business, then you will already have done a great deal to increase your chances of success.

Experience Note

The experience base contains examples of a range of justifications, some good and some not, for initiating reuse programmes.

- Conviction that reuse is essential in order to achieve a radical reduction in the software cost element of the company's products. 'If we do not achieve that reduction the competition will put us out of business.'

- Systematic assessment of the business opportunity for reuse (in terms of product line and market characteristics) and of the process potential for success with reuse.

- No systematic assessment, but instead an intuitive recognition of the business opportunity and the process potential.

- Wish to display technical leadership. This can have a genuine business value (the example was a software house).

- The Everest syndrome – climb the mountain because it's there: a response simply to the technical opportunity, without evaluating the business context.

- A wish to 'do objects', with reuse merely as a cover story.

5.3 Reuse for All, and All for Reuse

Any organization that is committed to a sustained programme of software process improvement (SPI) will desirably select one (or a few) improvement targets to act as a focus for improvement effort during a particular phase of its SPI programme. Examples of the kinds of topic that can act as a focus for improvement are configuration management, inspections, measurement, or project management. Another is reuse.

It is part of the message of this book that reuse should not be undertaken for its own sake, without setting it in a wider improvement context. A systematic reuse initiative should therefore be treated as a *reuse-focused SPI* initiative. Reuse may be the only SPI focus over a given period of time, or it may be one among several; an organization's ability to cope with several concurrent SPI focuses is often one measure of its process maturity.

Experience of SPI in many companies has led to the identification of a portfolio of success factors – principles that, if followed, are good predictors of success. Those success factors are as applicable to the introduction of reuse as they are to any improvement initiative.

One success factor that is absolute and primary is that any SPI initiative, whatever its focus, must win involvement from all managers and practitioners concerned with the process. That *total involvement* means that everyone must be aware of changes and the reasons for them, must accept them and be committed to their successful roll-out, and should feel ownership of them through having participated in designing them.

All empirical evidence indicates that such total involvement is achieved by companies that have succeeded with SPI, and that they recognize it as a primary ingredient of success. It is also a recognized key success factor in broader corporate change programmes, such as total quality management, business process reengineering, and the learning organization. Finally, within the limited scope of the SURPRISE survey, those ESSI reuse projects that have been successful have achieved total involvement, and acknowledge its critical importance.

The ability to achieve total involvement is highly dependent on the culture of an organization. Figure 5.4 sets out some of the cultural factors that can act as enablers for total involvement. That list of factors is not an unattainable ideal, recommended by some theoretical guru on the basis of abstract principles and no experience – all the attributes have been achieved in real companies undertaking real SPI initiatives (including reuse initiatives). You do not, however, have to achieve perfection in every success factor – it would almost certainly be impossible to find any organization that does.

Check your organization against the list. If some of the factors are absent for you, then consider carefully whether you need to initiate corrective changes to support you in achieving the goal of total involvement. One encouraging thing, however, is that you do not necessarily have to get the culture 100 per cent right before attempting any process change. Process change often itself acts as a catalyst to cultural change – there can be a synergy between the two. Thus, while it would be bad news if all or most of those cultural enablers were absent in your organization, the absence of just a few need be no problem, and a reuse introduction programme can act as a stimulus and support for achieving yet more cultural advance.

The real payoff from involving everyone is that reuse change is driven by the enthusiasm of the very people who have the best knowledge and the most

- Commitment to organizational learning through feedback from experience.
- A supportive no-blame culture, which renounces fear as a motivator, and in which challenges are welcomed and risks accepted.
- A high valuation on achieving consensus.
- Encouragement of a relentless search for improvement opportunities by everyone, supported by recognition award schemes.
- A knowledge-dissemination culture, using all possible communication channels to spread information.
- Widespread use of in-house awareness and training meetings, workshops and special interest groups, attended by everyone with a need to know.
- Leadership, and visible commitment to change, from the top down.
- Improvement topics becoming part of everyone's everyday language.
- Use of staff appraisals to gain commitment to change, and to review achievement against goals, at the individual level.
- Explaining the reasons for change, and its benefits both for the organization and for individuals (leading to feelings of added security rather than threat).
- Management actions to minimize both the amount and the effects of resistance to change (some resistance is probably inevitable).
- Focus on achieving early success stories, and giving them high internal visibility.
- Celebrating success (for instance with a party!).
- Fostering collaborative competition between teams in achieving change.
- Making sure that staff perceive change as helping them, not hindering them, and that it adds to their job satisfaction and pride in the quality of their work.
- Ensuring that change is carefully managed so that individuals are not overwhelmed by too much change happening at once.
- Absence of a paternalistic style, which offers a comfort blanket to staff because all decisions are taken by an all-wise management.

Fig. 5.4 Cultural enablers for total involvement.

99

direct experience of the processes affected by reuse. Their knowledge and experience is a key asset in adapting general principles of good practice to the particular circumstances of the individual organization, and making sure that the change really works. The contrast is with a management that decides on reuse, quite possibly for sound logical reasons, and simply imposes its adoption by decree, in the manner of an absentee landowner imposing some new agricultural method on a remote, uncomprehending and resisting peasantry.

Total involvement is a people-driven approach to process change. It recognizes that, however well designed processes may be, their success in terms of day-to-day enactment depends ultimately on people, and that an organization's people are its prime resource. It recognizes that, however powerful a technique such as reuse may be in theoretical terms, its potential will be lost unless it is understood and welcomed by the people who have to use it – unless it makes sense to them. Among the repertoire of high-potential improvement techniques, reuse suffers more than most from being wrapped in excessive technical mystique, preventing it from making sense to the majority of straightforward developers.

Experience Note

- The experience base indicates that it is easier to gain total involvement in a small unit or enterprise than a large one. Referring to two named companies, both of which have combined successful reuse with total involvement, **Chase** has always been small, whereas **Sodalia** was small at the time when it initiated reuse, has since grown substantially, but has nevertheless managed to retain total involvement.

- **Thomson-CSF** (a) embarked on reuse in the wider context of a relatively non-participative corporate culture, (b) recognized the need to change that culture in the case of the software groups undertaking reuse, and (c) successfully carried out the culture change to achieve total involvement within those groups.

- Another company started from a similar position to Thomson's, but reacted differently. Instead of an immediate culture change to allow reuse to move ahead rapidly, they opted to work within the cultural limitations and accept a more gradual reuse programme.

- The association between lack of total involvement and relative failure with reuse is quite strongly observable. In some cases it is specially noticeable that the reuse initiative started from middle management without any awareness or commitment from top management.

5.4 Adapting the Work Structure

You have decided that there is a business justification for the introduction of systematic software reuse, as a significant *strategic change*. You understand the need for total involvement, and for the *cultural change* (if any) that may be needed to achieve that. Having decided on the changes in strategy and culture, you must now address the need for *organizational change*, that will be synergistic with the strategic and cultural changes, each supporting the others.

This Section addresses the organizational change issues in general terms, suggesting a number of broad requirements and principles. Examples of specific organizational solutions, arrived at by individual enterprises in the light of their individual circumstances and goals, are to be found in the case histories in Chapters 8 and 9 later in this book.

Let us start with an overview of activities that need to be organized in a reuse initiative, during the initial transition (or take-up) phase and then in the subsequent phase of continuing practice. They may be partitioned into three levels, *strategic management, tactical management and technical leadership*, and *specialist support*, as shown in *Fig. 5.5*.

STRATEGIC MANAGEMENT
- Setting business goals for reuse.
- Establishing change strategy to achieve business goals.
- Determining performance indicators to track progress toward goals.
- Deciding resource allocation.

TACTICAL MANAGEMENT AND TECHNICAL LEADERSHIP
- Designing changes to existing software development practice.
- Planning the change process.
- Tracking implementation.
- Securing commitment to change.
- Ensuring skills availability and development.
- Organizing assessments.
- Achieving integration of existing and new practices.
- Establishing and monitoring detailed reuse metrics.
- Budgetary management.

TECHNICAL FUNCTIONS
- Reusable asset development.
- Reuse support.

Fig. 5.5 Key reuse activities.

The organizational requirement is to adapt an enterprise's existing work structure to accommodate activities of the kinds listed in the panel. We use the term work structure to mean the system of interrelated job descriptions for individuals, and terms of reference for teams and groups, that defines how an enterprise seeks to map its business goals and processes onto its available human resources. Adapting the work structure involves a combination of (a) changing existing job descriptions and terms of reference, and (b) creating new ones.

Note that a work structure is not the same thing as an organization chart. An organization chart relates to the work structure of an enterprise rather as the tip of an iceberg relates to the whole iceberg. Similarly, an organization chart shows only a fraction of the reality, which has far more detail and dynamism than can be captured in a formal chart (and which enterprises might not wish to display anyway!). An enterprise's work structure is the product of its size, diversity, history, management style, organizational philosophy, leaders' personality, etc., and there is an extent to which they can at best only be tacitly understood rather than explicitly defined.

There are no neatly packaged solutions to the question of how enterprises should adapt work structures to accommodate their varying approaches to reuse. Organizational problems are nevertheless of critical importance. Get the answers wrong, and the whole reuse initiative can fail, however strong the strategic commitment and technological competence. There are a number of roles that are intrinsic to the reuse process – either specific to it or impacted by it – as discussed already in Chapter 4. Those roles have to be performed, and must therefore be assigned in some way. Failure to assign them, or to assign them appropriately, will pose serious risk.

As well as being important, the organizational issues created by reuse can also be quite subtle, complex and difficult, both to appreciate and also to manage. It is hard to do justice to them in a limited space. We propose to approach them in two stages (see *Fig. 5.6*), first looking at six *conditioning factors* that are likely to influence how an enterprise structures its reuse efforts, and second identifying two *key decisions* that, in the light of those conditioning factors and other factors, need to be made about work structuring.

5.4.1 Conditioning Factors

The six conditioning factors listed in *Fig. 5.6* will now be discussed briefly in turn. By *conditioning factors*, we mean aspects of an enterprise's culture, business and way of working that are already in place, which have had a past influence in creating present work structures, and which will have an influence in how those work structures are now adapted to accommodate the

CONDITIONING FACTORS
- Single software development unit *vs* multiple units.
- Large *vs* small software development unit(s).
- Single application domain *vs* multiple domains.
- Full-time specialist individuals *vs* part-time specialist teams.
- SPI-led reuse *vs* reuse-led SPI.
- Change by large steps *vs* change by small steps.

KEY DECISIONS
- Separate *vs* integrated reusable asset development.
- Separate *vs* integrated reuse support.

Fig. 5.6 Organizational issues for reuse.

new and changed activities. Decisions will be conditioned less by any individual factor on its own, but more by the interactions between all of them taken together.

Single software development unit *vs* multiple units. Within an enterprise, software development may be undertaken by one or more distinct organizational units. (In the multiple-unit case, the units may or may not be at separate physical sites.) The existence of multiple units raises the question of whether the reuse initiative should encompass all units and, if so, whether its management and organization should be separate for each unit or integrated across them. An integrated reuse initiative covering multiple units requires additional work structures, in order to meet the needs for additional coordination and communication. In the extreme case, a large hierarchically structured corporate, with several levels of breakdown from the top through major operating divisions to individual business units, might need to 'shadow' those levels of breakdown in the structures it establishes to coordinate reuse as a corporate-wide initiative.

Large *vs* small software development units. Irrespective of whether there are one or more software development units in an enterprise, the unit size may vary. A large unit might be one with a hundred or more developers, a small unit one with 10 or less. Unit size is a powerful influencing factor on work structures. The bigger the unit, for instance, in general the greater is the likelihood of specialization among its members, and the more attention is necessary to achieving effective coordination and communication among them.

Single application domain *vs* multiple domains. The total software development effort within an enterprise may encompass one or more application domains. That is independent of the number and size of the units within which development effort is organized. An enterprise may, at one extreme, develop software for a single domain across several units or, at the opposite extreme, develop software for multiple domains in a single unit. Between those extremes, if several units develop software for several domains, there may or may not be a one-to-one mapping between units and domains.

Two examples of how work structuring can be influenced by mappings between units and domains are: (a) if a single domain is handled by more than one development unit, then the organization of domain-specific activities (such as domain modelling) takes more effort, because coordination between the units is necessary; (b) if more than one domain is handled by a single development unit, then the organization of horizontal (cross-domain) reuse is easier than if the domains are handled by different units.

Full-time specialist individuals *vs* part-time specialist teams. This factor is a matter of what might be called the *organizational style* of an enterprise, and refers to alternative approaches to the handling of specialist competences. In the software context, the issue is whether a specialist competence should be dispersed among 'generalist' development staff, who have different primary responsibilities and skills, or whether to concentrate it in the hands of a specialist individual or group for whom it will be their primary responsibility and skill. The decision partly depends on stylistic issues of whether the organization has a preference for skills partitioning, formal job descriptions and 'deep' hierarchies; it also partly depends on how intensively the competence needs to be deployed – whether the demand for it is sufficient to occupy most of the full-time effort of an individual or group.

SPI-led reuse *vs* reuse-led SPI. This is a very important factor. By 'SPI-led reuse' we mean the situation where a reuse initiative fits into an established long-term software process improvement programme. The opposite case, 'reuse-led SPI', is where reuse is the enterprise's first serious attempt at SPI, and emerges as the driver of a longer-term improvement programme.

In the case of SPI-led reuse, it can be expected that a work structure to provide management and support for SPI is already established. The main features of such a structure would normally include: (a) a *software process steering group* (or a linked hierarchical structure of such groups, up through the levels in a large hierarchically structured corporation), providing strategic management; (b) a *software engineering process group* (SEPG) (or one such group per development unit, in the multiple-unit case), providing tactical management and technical leadership; and (c) a number of *process specialist teams* (typically one per current improvement goal), each providing specialist technical support in its area of expertise. In an organization with multiple and/or large units, all three levels of organizational structures would normally exist as distinct entities; in a single small unit, there would be some merging of functions (for example a single group might act as both steering group and SEPG). Irrespective of size, different enterprises will take different approaches about whether membership of these groups should be full-time or part-time or a mixture (see the previous bullet).

Where such a structure is in place for SPI, a reuse initiative should fit into it, and should benefit from its accumulated experience of managing and supporting process change. Representation of the reuse initiative should be added to the steering group(s) (perhaps in the person of the reuse champion if one exists) and to the SEPG(s); and a reuse specialist team (possibly several in the multiple-unit case) should be established.

In the case of reuse-led SPI, such a structure will not already be in place. Obviously, a full-scale structure, of the kind described above, is not necessary initially to handle the single goal of reuse. But the assumption should be made that the reuse initiative will be the first phase in a longer-term SPI programme, and therefore that the reuse management and support structure should be established in such a way that it can grow over time to manage and support SPI as a whole. However it is organized, the need is to provide strategic management (through the equivalent of a steering group), tactical management and technical leadership (through the equivalent of an SEPG), and specialist technical support (through the equivalent of a reuse specialist team). In a small single unit, this might all be provided, for instance, by as few as two individuals (say one manager and one technical person), initially devoting only a part of their time.

Change by large steps *vs* change by small steps. This is a matter of an enterprise's management style with respect to change. 'Change by large steps' emphasises reaching a given change objective by planning a small number of large steps, in the expectation that each planned large step can be implemented with minimum deviation from plan. 'Change by small steps' is a deliberately experimental approach which recognizes the inherent unpredictability and riskiness of change, and seeks to break down the journey toward a given change objective into as many small steps as is reasonable, with the opportunity of learning from each small step and adapting subsequent steps in the light of feedback from experience.

Change by large steps can be attractive, especially to managers of the *machismo* school, because once the plan is in place it can be driven through with maximum efficiency. It does, however, run the risk that pressures to conform to plan will swamp indicators of the need to adapt. By contrast, change by small steps is explicitly willing to empower those affected by change in the unfolding change process, and to capitalize on their first-hand knowledge of the practices that are being modified.

The following are examples of ways in which the transition to reuse might be broken down into small steps. (a) Reuse might be introduced as a series of changes, each in a limited part of the development process and involving a limited number of asset types (for example assets in the technical domain, which are often easier to identify and reuse than those in an applications domain; or fine-grained assets, which are easier to specify than large-grained ones). (b) In a multiple-unit organization, a change might be piloted in one unit, before being rolled out to others. (c) A change might be piloted on one development project, one application domain, one product line or one client, before being rolled out to others.

Change by large steps tends to be a predominantly sequential process, with one large step following another – though of course the planning of step [i] may be concurrent with the implementation of step [i-1]. That need not be the case with change by small steps; pilot transitions of different kinds can be going on in different places at the same time.

Overall, change by small steps is to be preferred as being more adaptive and posing less risk. It has to be recognized, though, that it also demands more effort and competence in coordination and communication.

5.4.2 Key Decisions

The six conditioning factors described above influence how an enterprise will generally adapt its existing work structures of individuals, groups and project teams to cope with the whole range of reuse-related activities. We now turn to decisions about how to organize the central technical functions specific to reuse – reusable asset development, and reuse support. In each case, the essential choice is whether they should be *integrated* into the existing set of software activities, or provided by establishing new and *separate* work structures.

Separate *vs* integrated reusable asset development. The options are (a) to organize reusable asset development separately, effectively as an in-house 'reusable assets factory' providing products to the applications development teams (the producer-consumer paradigm), or (b) to integrate such work into the normal activity of applications development. Figure 5.7 shows factors that would favour option (a) – their absence would correspondingly favour option (b). The more of these factors are present, the stronger is the case for creating a separate organizational structure for developing reusable assets. Conversely, the fewer factors are present, the stronger is the case for integrating development for reuse with mainstream applications development.

- ... domain expertise is scarce. (It is a key resource that should not be diluted, and those who possess it should be able to practise it with minimum distraction.)
- ... it is possible to distinguish in advance between assets with reuse potential and those without reuse potential.
- ... it is determined that reusable assets should be developed to higher (or at least different) quality standards than non-reusable assets.
- ... assets will be reused across multiple applications projects, and especially if those projects are denied extra resources for developing reusable assets.
- ... the workload of developing reusable assets and the workload of developing non-reusable assets are reasonably balanced. (If reusable asset development strongly predominates, then development for reuse should probably be regarded as the norm for the applications developers. If non-reusable asset development strongly predominates, then development for reuse should probably be accommodated on an exception basis within normal development work.)
- ... the total volume of software development work is sufficiently large to justify creating separate organizational structures for normal applications development and development for reuse. (This may be called the critical mass condition.)
- ... the management style favours specialisation, skills partitioning, 'deep' organizational hierarchies and strong management control.

Fig. 5.7 Separate development of reusable assets is favoured if . . .

In practice, separation and integration do not represent two clearly distinct alternatives. In reality, there is a spectrum of organizational solutions. A company which has experimented with a number of different points on the spectrum is Hewlett-Packard, as reported in a paper by Danielle Fafchamps (Fafchamps, 1994)[5]. Hewlett-Packard is a very large software producer, which has adopted the producer–consumer paradigm for reuse and where the organizational style favours specialisation. Thus the options which they tried all favour separating reusable asset development and treating it as a specialist function, but to varying degrees. Fafchamps identified four approaches, which she termed 'lone producer', 'nested producer', 'pool producer' and 'team producer'. Each is briefly described in *Fig. 5.8*.

Based mainly on the reactions of the people involved in these different approaches, Fafchamps reports a preference for the fourth (team producer) option. Readers who are interested in the advantages and disadvantages of each option should consult Fafchamps' paper.

Where there is a separation between reusable asset development and applications development (producer–consumer paradigm), there needs to be a balance between producer push and consumer pull. It is natural that producers will want to push their 'goods', and there is nothing wrong with that in principle. What should be avoided is a combination of strong

- **Lone producer:** one reuse specialist is responsible for developing reusable assets for two or more application teams. There may be several such lone producers, depending on the number of applications teams and the volume of demand for reusable assets. Each reuse specialist serves several applications teams, while not being a member of any.
- **Nested producer:** each applications team may have a reuse specialist responsible for developing reusable assets for 'consumption' by that team. In principle, there could be more than a single reuse specialist per applications team. Each reuse specialist serves, and is a member of, one applications team.
- **Pool producer:** this is an extension of the nested producer structure, where two or more applications teams treat their reuse specialists as a shared resource. This can lead to a better balancing of workload between teams. Each reuse specialist is a member of one applications team, but helps to serve several.
- **Team producer:** in this case, development for reuse is carried out by one or more specialist producer teams, each serving one or more applications teams. The producer teams and the applications teams have the same organizational status. Each specialist is a member of one producer team.

Fig. 5.8 *Some organizational patterns tested by Hewlet-Packard.*

producer push and weak consumer pull, if the weak pull is caused by a mismatch between what the consumers need and what is being pushed at them, and if the dominant push leads to inappropriate asset reuse and ultimately to poor applications.

Separate *vs* **integrated reuse support.** Whatever decision is reached about the degree of separation or integration between development for reuse and applications development, there is a need for the provision of reuse support. Reuse support functions are summarized in *Fig. 5.9*.

- Operating reusable asset catalogue/repository, and assisting in its use.
- Selection, procurement, redocumentation and support of externally acquired reusable assets.
- Participation in reviews/inspections of reusable assets developed in-house.
- Quality assurance and acceptance testing of reusable assets.
- Maintenance of reusable assets.
- Collection and monitoring of reuse metrics.
- Technical advice to producers and consumers of reusable assets.
- Selection and procurement of reuse-related methods and tools.
- Reuse training, awareness and dissemination.
- Reporting to company management on reuse performance.

Fig. 5.9 *Reuse support functions.*

Any of those functions could either be assigned to a separate reuse support group, or integrated with existing functions in the software organization. As examples of integration, the asset catalogue/repository could be combined with existing library and configuration management functions; procurement of external assets, methods and tools could be combined with existing acquisition functions; reuse training could be combined with existing training; and so on. On the other hand, if a separate reuse support group is established, it might in extreme cases incorporate reusable asset development (as discussed in the previous bullet) in its brief.

Evidence from the experience base suggests that such decisions are indeed strongly influenced by the conditioning factors discussed earlier in this Section (predominantly size and organizational style). Those (few) that opted for central specialist groups, because it was part of their culture, were broadly successful with their reuse initiatives. Those (the majority) that opted against, again following their culture, included both successes and failures. It must be stressed, however, that the size of the experience base is too small to justify any generalizations, and in any case it would be hard to decide in a particular case how much this single decision contributed to success or failure.

Experience Note

Sodalia

- Single large unit, covering several application domains.
  - Separate development of reusable assets, but only in response to a notified need from an applications project.
  - Advantages: (a) the asset developer has an overall vision, and is more qualified to take into account different sources of requirements than a software engineer directly involved in a project; (b) this solution sets up a producer–consumer relationship within the company. It is a consumer-pull approach.
  - Disadvantages: applications developer objectives and asset developer objectives may diverge (for example with respect to schedule constraints or quality requirements).

- Separate reuse support (covering all the functions mentioned above).

  - Advantages: reuse overhead costs are isolated.

  - Disadvantages: risk of disconnecting reuse specialists from applications developers, and consequent loss of total involvement.

> **Thomson**
>
> - Separate large units, with one or several domains per unit; Common Efficiency Teams at corporate level, to define improvement strategies and to monitor reuse in the units.
>
> - Reusable asset development is integrated with applications development.
>
> - Separate reuse support at corporate level, covering reuse introduction, domain analysis, and metrics collection and aggregation.

5.4.3 Final Comments on Work Structure

In this Section, we have looked at some of the considerations that should be taken into account in designing the organizational changes necessary for reuse. We have deliberately not offered packaged recommendations, but rather concentrated on identifying the issues.

Whatever solutions are adopted, it is important that effort spent in reuse-related work should be recorded. (That tends to be easier where separate specialist groups exist.) That critical requirement should be taken as a constant, common to all work structure solutions. Effort metrics are basic to almost all other measurements of reuse performance and success. They are discussed, along with other metrics, in Chapter 6.

Finally, it is important to keep organizational issues in their proper perspective. Without an appropriate work structure – one that 'goes with the grain' of existing work structures and existing incentives mechanisms, and thus minimizes the risk of generating resistance – reuse will be disadvantaged at birth. But placing too much emphasis on organization, and making the design of work structures the driver of reuse introduction, will equally condemn the infant to a likely premature death. Appropriate organization, in other words, is necessary, but it is by no means sufficient.

References

1. Keen, P. (1997) *The Process Edge: Creating Value Where it Counts*. Harvard Business School Press.
2. Milano, G. (1997) Article in the *Sunday Times*, 21 September 1997.
3. Bennett Stewart III, G. (1991) *The Quest for Value: the EVA Management Guide*. Harper Business.
4. Copeland, T., Koller, T. and Murrin, J. (1995). *Valuation: Measuring and Managing the Value of Companies*. John Wiley.
5. Fafchamps, D. (1994) Organizational factors and reuse. *IEEE Software*, September 1994.

Reuse Metrics

6

ABSTRACT

What to measure and how? After having pointed out important issues to be measured, this Chapter proposes a measurement approach based on business goals (applying the GQM framework).

6.1 General Aspects of a Metrics Programme

What to measure? That should be the starting point of any measurement programme. Without answering that question first, the odds are that just numbers will be collected. Collecting numbers is easy. Producing useful measures is not, and many measurement programmes have failed because they did not realize the difference. The conceptual tools helpful in this task are a measurement framework to organize entities and a method to define and select measures of those entities.

Measurement tries to characterize attributes of entities (for instance the height of a person, or the speed of a car). Fenton and Pfleeger propose a measurement framework (Fenton and Pfleeger, 1997)[1] which classifies entities in the software domain as processes (for instance *eliciting requirements*), products (for instance the *requirements document*), and resources (for instance the *requirements analyst*, or the *word processor* used to write down requirements). Software measurement deals with characterizing attributes of software entities (for instance the *effort* for *eliciting requirements*, the *size* of the *requirements document*, or the *daily cost* of the *requirements analyst*).

Attributes can be internal, if they depend on a single entity (for instance *size),* or external, if they depend on a relationship between entities (for instance *productivity* depends on the analyst, the customer, the requirement process). Measures can be direct (if they are computed on a single attribute) or indirect (if they are computed on many attributes).

With such a measurement framework we know that a measurement programme has to identify what attributes of what entities have to be measured. Even a simple software process is made of hundreds of such attributes. Measuring them all is not possible because of cost/time constraints, and useless because not all attributes are interesting.

The Goal-Question-Metric (GQM) approach (Basili and Rombach, 1988)[2] is the conceptual tool widely used to guide the choice of useful measures from the large number of possible ones. We will present here the GQM variation from Lionel Briand (Briand *et al.*, 1997)[3], that provides templates to specify goals. Note that in this variation no questions are used.

A certain number of goals for the measurement programme should be stated. Successful measurement programmes start with a few goals, which may be refined and extended over time. Each goal is expressed in a standard template: purpose, attribute, entity, viewpoint and context. Purpose can be expressed as one of the following verbs: characterize, evaluate, predict, monitor, control or change. Table 6.1 shows an example.

For each goal, one or more measures are defined, or selected from the ones proposed in the literature. Table 6.2 shows an example.

The ideas of *context* and *viewpoint* are essential here. 'Quality of the requirements document' could be measured in a radically different way depending on whether the viewpoint is that of the requirements analyst, the project

Table 6.1 Example of goals in a metrics programme.

Goal	Purpose	Attribute	Entity	Viewpoint	Context
G1	Characterize	The quality	Of the requirements document	From the viewpoint of the customer	In the context of division A of company X
G2	Evaluate	The duration	Of the requirements elicitation process	From the viewpoint of the project manager	In the context of division B of company X

Table 6.2 Example of decomposing goals to metrics.

Goal	Measure
G1	M11 – Number of missing requirements identified after requirements elicitation M12 – Number of requirements changed after requirements elicitation
G2	M21 – Total effort spent in the requirements elicitation process M22 – Calendar duration of the requirements elicitation process

manager or the customer. In other words the GQM method stresses the point that measurement must be focused, with respect to not only the choice of what should be measured (goals) but also the specific way of measuring them (context and viewpoint).

The definition of goals and measures is the most difficult part of a measurement programme, but not the only one. Measures have to be computed from data, and data has to be collected, verified and stored. The practical point to be addressed in the measurement programme is how data is collected, when, and by whom. Data could be collected manually on paper forms, or automatically with tools. A specific person could be dedicated to collect, verify and store data. The computation of measures and their analysis could be done on a regular periodic basis or triggered by specific events.

For instance M11 and M12 require that someone (client? customer service? project manager? quality assurance?) records each problem with requirements (using a paper sheet? a form on a screen?). Someone (measurement manager? quality assurance?) should process each record (as soon as produced? each week? each month?), classify the problem (missing requirement? changed requirement? discard as false problem?), produce reports (missing requirements per project? per week? ...). Someone else again (project manager? senior management? ...) should read the reports and use them.

As a result of the choices made, procedures have to be described, responsibilities assigned, and tools designed and implemented. In general the measurement programme requires changes in the software process to provide for the collection and analysis of data and its effective use.

How much does a metrics programme, and specifically a reuse metrics programme, cost?

Two specific activities, and sources of cost, can be identified: introduction, and current use. In the introduction phase, goals and measures have to be defined, procedures, roles and responsibilities assigned, tools purchased and installed, training and motivation of staff performed. Clearly this phase requires important effort and commitment. During current use, a fairly negligible amount of time is required from all staff to collect data, and a possibly important effort is required from someone in some defined role to process and analyse data. This effort should not be underestimated. The case of data that accumulates while nobody uses it is not uncommon.

While a precise estimate of cost depends on the context of each company, it should be underlined that mature engineering disciplines rely on the pervasive, routine use of empirical investigation, measurement and models. Software production is condemned to remain a mysterious craft as long as such an approach is not used.

6.2 A Typical Reuse Metrics Programme

We describe here a reuse metrics programme, derived from typical goals (see Table 6.3) and using the most commonly accepted reuse metrics (see Table 6.4). We suppose a limited context: either an SME, or a single division of a large corporation that uses a single reuse repository. The relevant roles are the project manager and the reuse manager. For a comprehensive and pragmatic study on reuse metrics see Jeffrey Poulin (Poulin, 1996)[4]. His work has largely inspired this Chapter.

The entities we are dealing with, according to Fenton and Pfleeger's framework, are the following.

- Products: all software work products, in particular reuse-specific work products (assets, repository).

- Processes: all software processes, in particular reuse-specific processes as listed in Chapter 4 (asset production, asset usage, asset management . . .).

- Resources: all roles, in particular developers, project manager, reuse manager, senior management.

6.2.1 G1

Goal G1 addresses the need of a reuse manager to monitor reuse activity through the utilisation of the repository. The number of assets in the repository (M11) should be appropriate to earlier forecasts of reuse potential. A growing number of assets indicates that asset production is working. However, a large and growing value for M11 is not in itself an indicator of

Table 6.3 Goals for a reuse metrics programme.

Goal	Purpose	Attribute	Entity	Viewpoint	Context
G1	Characterize	The utilisation	Of the repository	From the point of view of the reuse manager	In the context of a division of the company
G2	Evaluate	The extent of reuse	In a project	From the point of view of the project manager and reuse manager	In the context of a division of the company
G3	Evaluate	The variation in cost	Of reusable assets	From the point of view of the reuse manager	In the context of a division of the company
G4	Evaluate	The economic aspects	Of the software process including reuse	From the point of view of senior management	In the context of the whole company
G5	Evaluate	The quality	Of reusable assets	From the point of view of reusers	In the context of a project
G6	Predict	The reusability	of reusable assets	From the point of view of the reuse manager	In the context of a division of the company

success. Reports from the literature suggest that small, focussed repositories work better than huge ones. Moreover, if M11 is used as the main indicator of success of the reuse programme, this will favour production of assets regardless of their actual reuse.

Developers access a repository for browsing its contents (M12) and possibly retrieving assets for reusing them (M13). A significant decrease in either measure alerts the reuse manager that something may be going wrong with the reuse programme. A high value for M12 with a low M13 could indicate that the repository is missing some needed assets. In this case M14 (the number of searches failed because the required asset is missing or because the search was ill defined) should be monitored too. Another explanation could be a lack of training for potential reusers on what the

Table 6.4 Decomposing goals to metrics in a reuse metrics programme.

Goal	Measure (Note: each measure is discussed below.)
G1	M11 – Number of assets in repository M12 – Number of accesses (only browsing, not retrieval) to repository per period M13 – Number of retrievals from repository per period M14 – Number of failed searches per period M15 – Cumulative number of reuses per asset M16 – Cumulative number of reuses for all assets in repository
G2	M21 – Reuse level per project (RL) M22 – Number of accesses (only browsing, not retrieval) to repository per project M23 – Number of retrievals from repository per project
G3	M31 – Relative cost of reuse (RCR) M32 – Relative cost of writing for reuse (RCWR)
G4	M41 – Payoff threshold M42 – Organization's return on investment (ROI)
G5	M51 – Reliability M52 – Understandability
G6	M61 – Functional completeness M62 – Portability

repository contains and the functions to access it. A low M12 explains a low M13 with a lack of motivation for searching in the repository from potential reusers.

M15 and the derived M16 are good indicators of how well the reuse programme is doing from a technical point of view. They are also the starting point for computing M41. The reuse manager should consider assets never reused for a long period. The reasons can be many: the asset is at the end of its life span (in this case the reuse manager could decide to delete it from the repository), or the asset is at the beginning of its life span (reuse is expected to be high in the future), or the asset belongs to a domain where no projects have been developed for a while. Considering the past reuse history of the asset, the expectation for its future reuse, the cost of retention of assets, and the preference for lean instead of huge repositories, the reuse manager will be able to decide whether to delete assets from the repository. If most assets are never reused a serious problem could exist in the reuse process, either on the producers' or on the consumers' side.

Measures for G1 are easy to collect automatically if the repository is automated (see Chapter 3). The reuse manager should check their trend regularly (say once per month) and take necessary action.

6.2.2 G2

G2 is concerned with understanding how a project reuses assets from a repository. This is of interest to the reuse manager (from the repository side) and to the project manager (from the project side) and corresponds to a technical (not economic) viewpoint. The M21 measure is the reuse level (RL), or reuse factor. Usually it is defined in the literature as

$$RL = \text{reused software} / \text{total software}$$

Note that this definition applies to software solely in the sense of code. This is not completely consistent with the point of view of this book (reusable assets may be any work product, not only code), but we propose this measure because it is popular and easy to use, and because no established measures exist that consider the whole range of assets. Also, if code work products are packaged with related workproducts (analysis, design, test cases), this measure partially takes into account the reuse of non-code workproducts.

Note also that it is a high-level definition, with many possible interpretations. It raises two major measurement issues. The first one concerns how to define reused software, which is discussed separately in the next Section. The second one concerns how to measure the size of software (both reused software and total software). Two possible choices are lines of code and function points. There is no right or wrong choice, but it is essential that the choice be consistent inside the company in all projects. If lines of code are chosen, since it is not a standardized measure, the company should define its own counting standard, or adopt the counting rules implemented in a commercial metrics tool.

This measure should be computed at the end of each project, by the project manager and staff, possibly with the assistance of the reuse manager to ensure consistency. A low reuse level on a project could underline a problem either on the project or on the repository side. Perhaps the project did not make any effort to search and use reusable assets, or the repository did not contain any useful assets for the project. Measure M22 (the same as M12, but computed on a project level) is defined to verify if the former hypothesis is true. If so, this is clearly a problem. The latter is not a problem if the project is an 'outsider' for which no reusable assets are provided in the repository. It is a problem if the project is a typical one for the organization.

Measure M23 is useful in two ways. Compared with M22 it gives an idea of the effort made to search for assets vs the number reused; compared with the reuse level it gives an idea of the granularity of reused assets (a high reuse level with a low M23 means that large-grained assets were reused).

M21 can also be used to estimate in advance the reuse level of a project. In the earlier phases of the project (at the end of requirements analysis, or at the end of high-level design) an estimated reuse level can be agreed on by the reuse manager and the project manager. The estimated reuse level is then compared with the actual level at the end of the project. The estimated reuse level has two important uses. One is to motivate the project to invest effort to achieve the estimated reuse level. The other is to estimate cost and duration for the project. As such, the estimated reuse level is an input variable in cost estimation models (see for instance Balda and Gustafson, 1990)[5].

Measures M22 and M23 are easy to compute if the repository is automated and supports measurement functions. M21 can be automated only partially. A tool is essential to compute the size measures from the components of the formula. Some effort is required to record the assets reused by a project, and to measure the size of each.

6.2.3 G3

Goal G3 represents the need of a reuse manager to know the cost of assets in the repository. This has two aspects, cost to produce and cost to reuse. M31, often called the relative cost of reuse (or RCR) in the literature, measures the cost of reusing an asset in comparison with the estimated development cost in the absence of the asset. M32, often called the relative cost of writing for reuse (or RCWR), measures the cost of developing an asset for reuse in comparison with the estimated cost of developing it for single use only. These measures allow a payoff analysis at the level of a single asset. If RCWR = 1.5 and RCR = 0.7, five reuses (1.5/0.3) are needed to pay for the initial investment in the reusable asset. Note that neither measure takes into account maintenance costs.

Poulin (Poulin, 1996)[4] reports from the literature values for RCR in the range 0.1 to 0.4, and for RCWR in the range 1.0 to 2.2. He suggests values of 0.2 and 1.5, respectively, as reasonable default values for simulations, equivalent to a payoff threshold of just under two uses (1.5/0.8). Nevertheless, each organization operates in a specific context, and should compute its own values.

The first step is computing the cost to develop non-reusable code work products. A number of past projects, not practising reuse, should be selected, and the total cost and number of code work products developed in each project should be computed or estimated. An average cost per code work product can then be derived. Note that here we are dealing with code work products, and not with all types of assets. The hypothesis is that the total cost of a code work product includes all the upstream and downstream costs of other work products (requirements, design, test design, test, etc.).

118

The next step is to compute cost to reuse assets (RCR) and to write for reuse (RCWR). This requires a precise accounting of effort spent by developers in all phases (analysis, design, coding, testing, documentation, etc.) to develop reusable and non-reusable assets, and the effort spent to reuse assets. The problem here is that effort accounting systems used by most companies collect, at most, effort (then cost) dedicated to projects, not to assets. When a reuse programme starts, these accounting systems should be modified to collect effort and cost at the level of assets, and assets should be tagged as 'reusable', 'not reusable' or 'reused'. Given these modifications, at the end of each project it is possible to compute cost per asset, then RCR and RCWR.

If a team is specifically dedicated to the development of reusable assets, the task of identifying reuse-related effort is made easier. The cost of this team, divided by the number of reusable assets produced, compared with the cost to produce non-reusable code work products, leads easily to RCWR. Note that imprecision is introduced because code work products are compared with assets. This can be avoided only if a very precise accounting system is in place before introducing reuse.

If the effort accounting system cannot be modified, and only cost at the project level is available, the following approach may be adopted.

Considering projects that reuse code products but do not produce reusable code work products:

$$\text{total cost} = \text{new code cost} * (1 - RL) * \text{total software} +$$
$$RCR * \text{new code cost} * RL * \text{total software}$$

Given that total cost, RL (reuse level), new code cost and total software are known, the formula can be resolved to compute RCR. Total software is a measure of the size of the software developed, and should be expressed in the same units as RL (lines of code, function points, number of assets etc.).

RCWR can be computed in a similar way, provided that a group, or project, is explicitly dedicated to writing reusable assets.

RCWR should be updated each time a new asset is introduced to the repository. The reuse manager should receive from developers the figures of effort for developing the asset, assess if the figures are reliable, and update RCWR. RCR should be updated at the end of each project. Again, the reuse manager receives figures from the development team, assesses them and updates RCR.

6.2.4 G4

G4 expresses the point of view of senior management, interested in the economic aspect of reuse, specifically if and how much reuse reduces costs.

Sometimes the driver for introducing reuse is not reduction of cost, but reduction of time to market, or increase in quality. In these cases other measures should be used (for example project lead time, or defect density delivered to the customer). A variation of G4 is Predict instead of Evaluate. The following measures and models can be used alternatively to predict economic trends. The economic analysis can be made at the level either of an individual asset, or at the level of the whole reuse process.

The payoff threshold (M41) (Gaffney and Durek, 1989)[6] takes the asset point of view, and computes the number of reuses needed to pay for the initial cost of developing it. The threshold can be computed using the following formula, where RCWR is the investment, and (1-RCR) is the return.

$$\text{Payoff threshold} = \text{RCWR} / (1\text{-RCR})$$

The formula can be computed for each asset, then compared with the number of reuses of the asset. In practice this level of detail is not always necessary and requires a sophisticated data collection system. Therefore the typical use of the formula is with average values of RCWR and RCR, and gives an average payoff threshold. Note that this measure takes into account only direct development costs and savings. It takes no account of the overheads of the reuse programme or of maintenance savings.

If the whole reuse process is considered, at the level of an entire organization, M42 computes the Return on Investment (Organizational ROI, adapted from Jeffrey Poulin (Poulin (1996)[4]).

Let's consider first the investment required to develop reusable assets, and to manage and maintain them.

$$I \text{ (investment)} = \text{RCWR} * \text{(size of reusable code)} *$$
$$\text{(cost of new development per unit of size)}$$
$$+ \text{(size of reusable code)} * \text{(cost of maintenance per unit of size)}$$

Then, if we consider a single project, the savings S in development and in maintenance are

$$S = (1\text{-RCR}) * \text{RL} * \text{(size of developed code)} *$$
$$\text{(cost of new development per unit of size)}$$
$$+ \text{RL} * \text{(size of developed code)} * \text{(cost of maintenance per unit of size)}$$

Last, let us consider all projects of the company:

$$\text{ROI} = \Sigma_i \, S_i - I$$

Note that this formula sums over many projects, and therefore considers a substantial time period. A more precise model could take into account the discounted cash flow using net present value techniques.

6.2.5 G5

There is a relationship between the quality of an asset and its reuse. A potential reuser of an asset is more likely to reuse it if (s)he can understand what the asset does, and if (s)he believes the asset does it reliably. Quality, in this context, thus means reliability and understandability. G5 represents the specific point of view of the developer, or potential reuser of an asset, and what (s)he expects from it. The same point of view should be taken by the reuse manager, when (s)he accepts assets for the repository (the subprocess *Test and Qualification*, within the process Asset Production: see Chapter 4). We propose two high-level measures for G5, that should be specialized further depending on the function of the specific work products.

M51, reliability, expresses the level of confidence in the ability of the asset to perform its declared function. In the case of code work products this could be further decomposed to measures such as *test coverage, defects found in the test phase,* or *defects found after release*. In the case of other types of work products, similar measures should be defined. For all types of work products, reliability is a function of the quality assurance activities (inspections, reviews) performed on them during the development process. Also, for all types of work products, a further reliability level is introduced if the reuse manager submits them to a further validation before accepting the asset for the repository. The reuse manager could present to potential reusers an aggregated view of M51, such as high, medium or low reliability, along with a definition of what high, medium and low mean in terms of the work product considered and the lower-level measures used. The potential reuser could select only assets above a defined reliability threshold for a specific project.

M52, understandability, expresses the readability and completeness of the description of the asset in the catalogue, and of the work products in its body. From a pragmatic point of view, no measures are really useful here. The reuse manager should assess and improve readability and completeness based on feedback from developers. Next, understandability depends on the extent to which the asset depends on other assets. In the case of code, a useful measure could be a simplified fan-in/fan-out measure, such as the number of procedures called by a reusable procedure, or the number of classes used by a reusable class. If the reuser is allowed to access the code work product (white or grey box reuse), the complexity (for instance the cyclomatic complexity) of the code work product can be another useful measure.

As in the case of M51, the reuse manager could present to potential reusers an aggregated view of M52, such as high, medium or low understandability, and a definition of what high, medium and low mean in terms of the work product considered and the lower-level measures used. All measures related to G5 should be collected or computed by the reuse manager when the asset is accepted for the repository, attached to the asset, and modified as needed.

6.2.6 G6

G6 tries to measure the reuse potential of an asset. It represents the point of view of the reuse manager in deciding whether to accept the asset into the repository or not. Different aspects of the asset have to be evaluated.

- Internal attributes related to the quality of the asset, such as reliability and understandability. These are the same attributes considered by G5. As for G5, the hypothesis is that the reuse potential is higher if the potential reuser can more easily understand and trust the asset.

- External attributes such as functional completeness (M61) and portability (M62). *Functional completeness* is the degree to which the asset has the required functions for its expressed requirement, and for any reasonable future requirement. *Portability* is the ease of porting the code part of the asset to a different hardware and/or software environment.

M62 and especially M61 are predictive measures, and in fact the purpose of G6 is to predict. *Predictive* goals are much more difficult to measure than *evaluate* and *characterize* goals, as they depend on predictive models that have to be built and validated for specific contexts of usage. On the other hand, note that M15 provides an *a posteriori* measure of the actual reuse of an asset. The predictive model should be validated on the basis of M15, when this becomes available for the asset.

G6 corresponds to a very simplified view of reusability. More comprehensive reusability models, such as the one of REBOOT (Karlsson, 1995)[7] include a greater number of attributes. In particular reusability depends also on its *usefulness,* or on how well it fits the domain of a reuse application. To put it simply, just because an asset is of top quality (in the sense of reliability and understandability) and functionally complete does not mean in itself that it is reusable. The asset will be reused only if it proves useful in the context of a future application.

No established ways of measuring usefulness are available today. Judgement is used instead.

6.2.7 What To Count as Reused?

The reuse level measure requires a precise agreement on what should be counted as reuse, and what should not. There is no standard definition: each organization should decide on one, and use it consistently. While absolute values of the measure may not be meaningful, variations observed across projects can be meaningful and useful. For the same reason, comparison among reuse levels in different companies should not be made, unless the definition is known and is the same. Of course this applies also within a single company, if reuse level is computed in different ways in different departments or divisions.

In the context we are using for our typical metrics programme – a reuse repository to be exploited by all projects of a division of a company, or by all projects of an SME – the precise definition could take the following form.

A reused asset is any asset used, without modifications, to build, directly or indirectly, the product developed in a given project, and coming from the repository. The asset should be counted once per project, even if it is reused many times in it.

The important points in this definition, that actually express a concept of reuse, are as follows.

- *Any asset used*: as an asset is made of description and body, *asset* means any work product part of the body of the asset. In the typical case, the work products of a reused asset are analysis document, design document, source code and test cases. *Used* means that the reuser understands in detail what the asset does by reading the analysis and design documents, writes calls to the source code in the application (s)he is writing, compiles and links the source code, and runs the test cases. In another case the asset might not contain code in the body, and the body could be composed of a domain analysis document only; in this case *used* means that the reuser reads the document and uses it to produce other work products in the application (s)he is developing.

- *Without modification*: if any work product of the asset is modified, it does not count as reused. The definition thus assumes black box reuse.

- *To build directly or indirectly*: the reused asset should be included in the final product directly as part of it, or indirectly with tools used to develop the product. The latter refers, for example, to testbenches developed to test embedded software, but not shipped, or to analysis and design work products.

- *Coming from the repository*: assets not coming from the repository are not counted as reused. This point marks the difference between ad hoc and systematic reuse. Only assets accepted in the repository, properly developed, qualified and documented are 'official' assets. As a corollary, calls to operating system, database, network or GUI primitives are not counted, as far as these functions are available free and not explicitly developed for the repository. On the other hand, COTS assets explicitly evaluated, purchased, classified and inserted in the repository are counted. Moreover, assets coming from the project itself are not counted. This latter approach is called also internal reuse. The logic for excluding internal reuse is that identifying modules and using them many times is simply a good design practice that each project should use by default, without any need for systematic reuse and repositories.

- *Counted once*: the logic for this choice is to favour good design practices and a fair economic approach. Let's suppose the asset is not reused from the repository, but developed in the project and used many times in it. Good design practice suggests that the designer notices the need for the asset, uses it wherever needed, but develops it only once. For the same reason, if the asset comes from the repository, it should be counted only once.

While the above definition is only illustrative, and is not by any means the only possible one, it supports quite a rigorous concept of reuse based on a repository, with the overall purpose of encouraging the production of reusable assets and their disciplined reuse. It should be clear from the points discussed above that a looser definition of reuse level can give extraordinarily different values for the very same project. Or, quoting Watts Humphrey, 'You can get almost any numbers you want . . . by changing the way you count'.

Experience Note

Very few of the projects in the experience base satisfied the definition of reuse given above. Most of them allowed (and practised) reuse with modification of assets (most of the time code work products). In general, very few of them collected reuse metrics. The reasons identified for this situation are:

- few companies have a metrics programme at all;

- therefore few have a baseline of effort and quality against which to compare reuse projects;

- the interest in an economic analysis of the effects of reuse is low.

When measures are collected, they are usually a subset of the ones presented in this Chapter. Sodalia reports a cumulative number of reuses per asset (M15) in the range 1 to 5. Eliop reports an RCWR value of 1.6, and an RCR of 0.2.

Experience Note

Thomson ATC uses a product line approach. A general purpose product is developed, then customized to fit the need of each client. In this case the goal of the metrics programme is to monitor how well the general purpose product is engineered to satisfy different but similar needs. So the measures below are quite different from the ones presented above. This should not surprise the reader, but convince him/her even more of the usefulness of a GQM approach to define a metrics programme.

Let's call GP the general purpose product, and C the customization for a client. The code in C is divided into two parts: what is reused from GP (ReuseGP), and what is added (NewC). The code in GP is also divided into two parts: what is reused (ReuseGP), and what is not reused (DeletedGP = GP – ReuseGP).

RL = ReuseGP / C

GPUF = ReuseGP / GP [utilization factor, indicates how well GP captures the commonalities among applications]

C distance = NewC / GP [indicates the variability of each application]

Three extreme scenarios are possible, analysing the indicators across several customizations.

GP and C overlap (high RL, high GPUF, low C distance). Commonality among applications is very high, GP captures this commonality.

GP and C do not overlap (low RL, low GPUF, high C distance). Commonality among applications should be assessed, GP does not capture this commonality.

GP subset of C (high RL, high GPUF, high C distance). GP could be extended to capture more of the commonality among applications.

References

1. Fenton, N. and Lawrence Pfleeger, S. (1997) *Software Metrics: a rigorous and Practical Approach*, 2nd edn. PWS Publishing.

2. Basili, V.B. and Rombach, H.D. (1988) The TAME Project: Towards Improvement–Oriented Software Environments, *IEEE Trans. on Software Engineering*, 14(6), June 88.

3. Briand, L.C., Differding, C.M. and Rombach, H.D. (1997) Practical Guidelines for Measurement-Based Process Improvement, *Software Process Improvement and Practice*, 2(4) 1997.

4. Poulin, J.S. (1996) *Measuring Software Reuse*, Addison Wesley.

5. Balda, D.M. and Gustafson, D.A. (1990) Cost Estimation Models for the Reuse and Prototype Software Development Lifecycles, *ACM SIGSOFT Software Engineering Notes*, Vol. 15, N.3, July 1990, pp. 42–50.

6. Gaffney, J.E. and Durek, T. (1988) Software Reuse – Key to Enhanced Productivity, Software Productivity Consortium, SPC-TR-88–015, April 1988.

7. Karlsson, E.A. (editor) (1995) *Software Reuse*, John Wiley & Sons.

Reuse Techniques and Technologies

7

ABSTRACT

Several techniques have been proposed to maximize the reuse of components, of architectural designs, and even of the software designers' experience in solving domain-specific problems. These techniques are partial in their life-cycle coverage and in the viewpoints that they represent. This Chapter reviews the contributions and usefulness of some of these techniques.

7.1 Rationale

The aim of the Chapter is to present the most relevant techniques for building and using reusable software assets. For that reason, the structure of the Chapter reflects the relationships between the techniques.

Section 7.2 presents several types of *architectures*, and discusses how they facilitate reuse, from traditional monolithic and client/server, to multi-tier and internet architectures. This Section provides the overall context for the various techniques introduced in the subsequent Sections.

Section 7.3 describes *object-oriented techniques* (OOT), with specific reference to OO analysis (OOA), OO design (OOD) and OO programming (OOP).

Sections 7.4 to 7.6 describe techniques which have emerged from the OO world, namely *design patterns*, *OO frameworks*, and *component-based development*. These three Sections contain dependencies on each other and on

Section 7.3. In particular, design patterns are an attempt to overcome the limitation of the pure code reuse of the class library approach by emphasising the importance of design reuse. OO frameworks are an attempt to combine code reuse (class libraries) with design reuse (design patterns). Component-based development is an attempt to reduce the complexity of OO framework use and reuse: a component is a black-box building block with a well defined interface and an internal complexity that can range from a simple class to a complete framework. Section 7.6 discusses different types of components: client-side components, server-side components, and what can be considered as an emerging type of component, coming from internet architectures.

Section 7.7 describes software agents, which constitute an interesting and promising reuse technique.

For the above techniques, a list of enabling methodologies and technologies is presented where appropriate. They include UML (for OOA and OOD), CORBA and DCOM/COM+ (for OO frameworks), and Enterprise JavaBeans, Java Beans and ActiveX (for component-based development). XML and internet components will also be addressed when dealing with internet architectures.

Finally, Section 7.8 offers a comparison of these techniques and draws conclusions.

7.2 Reuse-Enabling Architectures

Let us start with an overview of some major types of architectures that will give us the global picture. An architecture is defined in terms of identified system components, how they are connected, and the nature of those connections (protocols for communication, synchronization and data access). It is fundamental to have an understanding of architectures because they determine the types of technologies used to build software systems, the types of components involved, and the processes for building and reusing components.

A number of general-purpose architectures frequently occur, such as pipes/filters, client/server, three-tier, and layered. Some domain-specific architectures have also been identified, such as the subsumption architecture for mobile robotics.

Software architecture development has shifted attention from code reuse to design reuse, by giving more importance to the fundamental role that patterns of relationships between the elements of an architecture have in any design (see Section 7.4 on patterns). In contrast to the class library approach, the structure of interconnections between components is reused, rather than just the components themselves.

Software architecture reuse is based on the definition of 'architectural styles', that is descriptions of families of architectural designs that share a set of common assumptions (Abowd, 1993). An architectural style provides a specialized component vocabulary (for example client, server, application server), a connector vocabulary (for example pipe, data stream, request, service) and a set of rules and protocols for building specific topologies using components and connectors (for example, IIOP, HTTP).

Architectural styles improve communication between designers, who can refer to a shared terminology for reusing design solutions. Unfortunately, systematic reuse of concrete architectures and designs is more difficult than code-level reuse, since a design is not worth much in itself as a reusable artefact; the design, with its tradeoffs and consequences, must be understood by the reuser so that any necessary adaptations and changes can be made. Since software architectures are usually domain-independent, no guidance is given to the developer on choosing the right architecture for a specific application.

7.2.1 Three-Tier Architecture

The three-tier architecture (*Fig. 7.1*) is an evolution of the traditional two-tier client/server model. It is particularly well suited for large business applications, where several clients access one or more distributed databases.

The main difference between the two-tier and three-tier models is that in a three-tier architecture most of the business logic is not part of the client application, and is not implemented in the database as triggers and stored procedures, but is separated out in a middle layer called the business server. Business servers (tier 2) are independent from the application presentation (tier 1) and the types of clients, as well as from the databases (tier 3).

The client tier is responsible for the GUI (graphical user interface) and the presentation logic. The business server tier is responsible for the implementation of business processes (for example credit delivery, account management), business concepts (account, customer, credit) and the business rules that apply to them. The data access tier is responsible for storing the data and for giving access to the data independently of its location and its physical schema. Different client applications can access a given business server, and different business servers can access the same database.

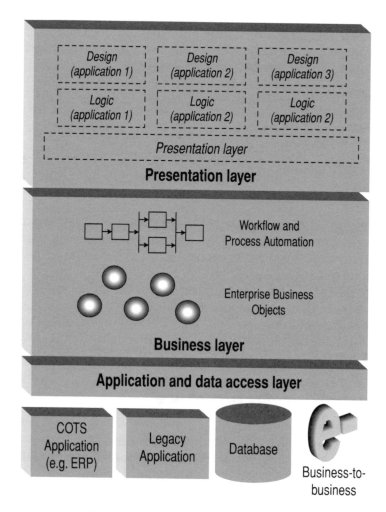

Fig. 7.1 Three-tier client/server architecture.

Three-tier architectures promise better reusability, scalability, maintainability and portability than the traditional two-tier model because they focus on business objects, whereas the two-tier model is often limited to the reuse of client-side low-level GUI components. However, the further architectural subdivision increases development complexity.

Section 7.6 will discuss in more detail business server-side components, and technologies like EJB and DCOM/COM+ that support them, as well as client-side GUI components implemented with JavaBeans or ActiveX.

7.2.2 Multi-Layered, Web-Enabled Architecture

As *Fig. 7.1* suggests, three-tier architectures can be developed into multi-tier architectures by subdividing each layer into several sub-layers. For instance, for low-coupling purposes, the data layer can be split into data access and data storage. If we consider that a database is not the only source of data, additional layers can be added to access legacy systems, COTS (commercial off-the-shelf) applications such as ERP (Enterprise Resource Planning), CRM (Customer Relationship Management) and internet systems. With the development of the internet, layered architectures had to be adapted to enable software systems to be open to the internet and accessible from internet browsers. The presentation layer can also be split, by distinguishing the presentation logic (what to diplay and when, what to display next etc.) from the graphical design (design of the web pages, windows, forms etc.). The business layer is also often subdivided into business entities and business processes (rules, workflows).

This type of 'web-enabled' system not only provides universal access to the information system from standard internet browsers, with the great advantage of avoiding the installation of application-specific software on the client, thus making the roll-out and maintenance processes much easier; it also gives access to data and applications from other business information systems through the internet ('B2B', or business-to-business).

7.2.3 Internet Systems Architectures

The internet and associated standards (HTTP: hyper-text transport protocol; HTML: hyper-text markup language; XML: eXtensible Markup Language) have provided a completely open and flexible model. It is leading to a new conception of information systems, not confined to one single enterprise but allowing the federation of several information systems through the internet. This applies to enterprise portals for businesses as well as to consumer portals. In both cases, such portals provide single unified access to multiple heterogenous information sources from several web sites, several information systems and several companies.

Such portals are made of several components, each of them providing access to a particular service: news, entertainment, travel, sport etc. for a consumer portal and business applications such as ERP, CRM and business intelligence systems for an enterprise portal. In addition, both types of portals often use common components like forums, newsgroups, chat and document management. Both those two types of portals are called 'horizontal', as opposed to 'vertical' or business-specific portals, which have similar architectures (*Fig. 7.2*) but target specific marketplaces, and use

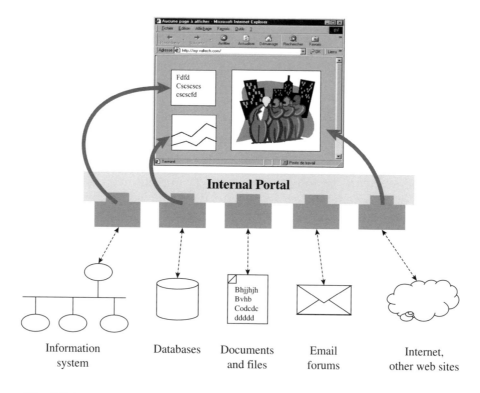

Fig. 7.2 Integration into the web browser: example of an internet portal architecture.

additional e-commerce components (for product catalogues, payment, auctions, etc.).

Besides the fact that portals are made of reusable components, they also make information accessible in standard formats (HTML, XML) from many sources. The difference between reusing the components that manipulate and give access to information on the internet, and reusing the information itself, becomes fuzzy. The broad availability of unlimited sources of information makes it possible to look at systems architecture differently, focusing on the integration of information sources on the client's browser instead of focusing on back-end integration. Internet systems have thus introduced a new paradigm, of building highly generic and reusable systems and components that process information in standard format, and integrating these components and this information in the end-user's personalized web page, instead of building systems made of specialized components integrated in the back-end. Web personalization and profiling techniques make it possible to compensate for the fact that components are very generic.

The concept of internet components will be developed further in Section 7.6.

7.3 Object-Oriented Techniques

Object-oriented techniques (OOT) provide methods and mechanisms for structuring models and program code to correspond to the objects (concepts) found in the problem domain. For example, in the business application domain, objects can describe a customer or a bank account, by means of attributes (such as account number), behaviours (such as issuing an account balance) and relationships between objects (such as an account belonging to a customer).

Compared with traditional procedural programming, OOT has the advantage of allowing the development of highly modular systems. This is accomplished by means of a set of principles such as information hiding and data abstraction. An application is no longer seen as a complex function that has to be decomposed into subroutines following a pure top-down approach. Instead, the designer identifies the main entities of the application domain, and their responsibilities and relationships, and designs the application having in mind which objects can be reused .

OOT consists of analysis (OO analysis, OOA), design (OO design, OOD) and implementation (OO programming, OOP).

Object-oriented analysis is concerned with the analysis of a system using object-oriented techniques. OOA methods provide modelling elements and relationships that allow analysts to capture everything of importance in a system. They encourage analysts to represent systems in the same way that they are perceived, without being constrained by how they will be implemented.

Object-oriented design is concerned with the transformation of OOA models into design models with desirable design properties.

Several OOA and OOD methods have been proposed in the literature, such as Booch (Booch, 1991) and OMT (Rumbaugh, 1991). The Unified Modeling Language (UML) (CetusLinks; UML) offers a standard language for specifying, visualizing, constructing and documenting the artefacts of software systems; it is method-independent. The Unified Process provides a process framework for interactive development based on OO modelling with UML. Both standards, UML and UP, have been adopted by the Object Management Group (OMG) and a very large community of players in the software market. Several software engineering tools that enable analysts and designers to capture object-oriented modelling and design decisions in graphic form are available on the market [CetusLink].

The basis of object-oriented programming is the concept of objects as program units which encapsulate both data and algorithms. This concept distinguishes the OOP paradigm from procedural and functional paradigms: the code which accesses and modifies given pieces of data is confined to one location in the program and is not spread uncontrollably throughout the program. Objects with similar properties are grouped into classes. For example, the class ACCOUNT might define a family of bank account objects, which differ from each other in terms of their specific account number, balance and owner.

OOP supports reuse in the form of class libraries by means of a set of techniques such as encapsulation, inheritance and polymorphism. Developers build applications by reusing library classes in two different ways. One consists of constructing new classes around the objects of existing classes. For example, the class BANK might encapsulate several objects of classes ACCOUNT and CUSTOMER. The other consists of deriving new classes as specialisations of existing ones. For example, the class SAVINGSACCOUNT might extend the class ACCOUNT by including the attribute 'interest rate'. Several programming languages and environments are available to the programmer for building and reusing class libraries. Examples can be found in CetusLink.

As explained in Section 2.4, a fundamental misconception relates OOT and reuse. In fact, the class library approach has not been much more successful in achieving effective reuse than the subroutine libraries of procedural languages; most of the successful class libraries consist of simple general-purpose container or collection classes which are object-oriented implementations of basic data structures.

The failure of the class library approach in achieving successful reuse is mainly due to the fact that it does not support systematic reuse of architecture and design in any way. In fact, as software systems continue to grow in size and complexity, architecture and design represent an increasingly large part of software development effort.

Design patterns, OO frameworks and component-based development are emerging techniques which promote not only code reuse but also analysis and design reuse. They will be discussed and compared in the following Sections.

7.4 Design Patterns

Several years ago, design patterns (CACM, 96) emerged from the object-oriented world as a technique for documenting design solutions. The most general definition of a pattern is a literary form, which describes an application *Context*, a design *Problem* which occurs in that context, and a *Solution* to the problem which has been proved by experience to be effective. Some authors extend the descriptions of their patterns by including other paragraphs: the opposing *Forces* and tradeoffs which the pattern resolves; an *Example*, which shows how the pattern has been applied in a specific case; and the *Implementation*, which describes techniques for implementing the pattern.

A pattern documents a concrete reusable solution to a recurrent architectural problem. A number of 'design pattern libraries' have been already defined, where by 'library" we mean a book or a paper that describes one or more design patterns: see for example the book by Erich Gamma et al (Gamma, 1995). The developer selects the design pattern which is most applicable to the problem in question (*Fig. 7.3*), and reuses the corresponding *Solution*. The *Context* and *Problem* sections of the pattern form make it easy for the developer to retrieve the right pattern. Craig Larman (Larman, 1998) provides a good approach to OO modelling with design patterns.

Patterns cover the range from analysis and overall program architecture to very specific details of physical design or implementation. A structured

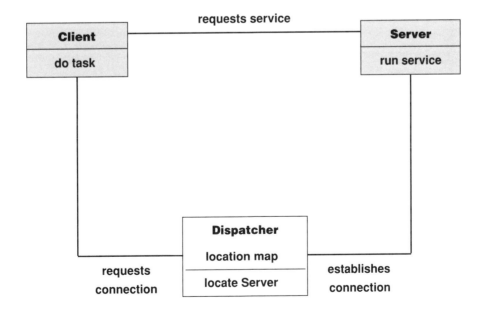

Fig. 7.3 Pattern client–dispatcher–server, (Buschmann, 1996).

collection of design patterns for a specific application domain is called a *pattern language*. The pattern language structure is represented by the dependencies between each pattern. For instance, a pattern for a low-level design problem usually depends on the previous application of more general patterns. Each pattern in the language represents a decision point: the choice whether to apply one pattern determines which patterns to consider next.

Patterns and pattern languages are concrete representations of domain expertise. They greatly raise the level of communication between designers working together. Each pattern is given a name, capturing its essence; pattern names then become part of the designers' vocabulary, allowing them to refer to complex problems and solutions with a single word, with less possibility of misunderstanding. Patterns are applicable not only to design but also to analysis. Analysis patterns (Fowler, 1995) are a way of reusing modelling expertise specific to a given business domain (such as modelling financial instruments).

Unfortunately, design patterns do not support code reuse in a systematic way, as class libraries do: the *Implementation* paragraph is very often missing, or just sketches a description in a high-level language. Usually, an existing class library hardly fits the solutions provided by a pattern language unless they are initially conceived to support each other. Design patterns and pattern languages, however, are very useful when the application has to be implemented from scratch.

7.5 Object-Oriented Frameworks

A framework is an integrated set of reusable and extensible software arte-facts for a specific application domain: a survey (CACM, 1997) is available. In object-oriented programming, a framework is expressed as a set of classes and relations describing structures of cooperating objects.

Concrete applications are generated by customizing the variable aspects of the framework. There are basically two kinds of framework customization.

- Black-box customization: the framework provides a specific implementa-tion of each variable aspect. The user generates an application by selecting the specific components to be plugged in into the framework structure (for instance the different toolbars in *Fig. 7.4*).

- White-box customization: the framework provides a generic implemen-tation of each variable aspect, which the user specializes for concrete

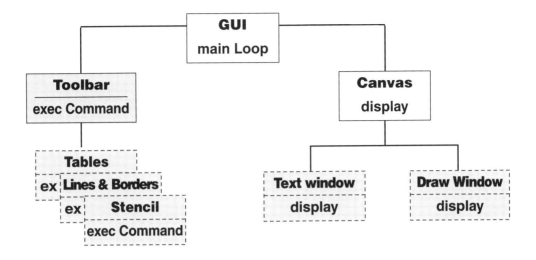

Fig. 7.4 Framework customization.

applications (for instance the canvas in *Fig. 7.4*). This kind of customization is more flexible, but requires deeper understanding of the framework design and implementation.

Both kinds of customization are frequently available in the same framework.

The traditional software life cycle from user requirements to final implementation and testing now becomes divided into two distinct main phases.

- Application framework development. This phase starts with domain analysis and produces the framework architectures and a set of reusable software artefacts (class aggregates). Usually, the framework is built by generalizing from a set of existing applications in the same domain and by exploiting domain analysis results.

- Concrete application development. This phase starts from the user requirements and consists of the framework customization. Usually, application testing and maintenance induces an extension of the original framework.

In contrast to most other reuse techniques, such as class libraries and design patterns, a framework consists of both reusable code and reusable design. That means that applications which are built using the framework are never designed from scratch; instead, the framework design is used as a starting point.

Building a reusable framework is usually difficult. It requires a deep understanding of the application domain for which it has been conceived, in terms of the entities and relationships that can be captured and reused. The more concrete the software artefacts are, the more specific their interactions become, and the harder it is for them to meet the requirements of future applications. Flexibility in the patterns of interactions between software artefacts is mandatory for the reusability of the framework. For this reason, frameworks are often built according to several design patterns.

OO frameworks can be classified into two categories.

● Application (or business or vertical) frameworks.

● Middleware (or horizontal) frameworks.

An application framework is a semi-complete application, which allows the development of a family of similar applications in a specific domain. In this sense, an application framework is more than a class library: most of the difficult design and analysis problems characteristic of the specific application domain have already been solved. Their characteristic is the so-called 'inversion of control': the framework provides the application architecture and the main control flow, which defines how the user-provided components are executed. The developer builds a new application by customizing the variable aspects of the framework. Usually an application framework supports both white-box and black-box customization. White-box customization requires a deep understanding of the framework. The SEMATECH Framework (Dosher, 1997) is an example of an application framework for the manufacturing domain.

A middleware framework consists of an integrated set of components which offer specific services, commonly used by a family of similar applications. As an example, the TINA Framework (TINA, 1995) offers a set of services for telecommunication applications, such as user authentication, session control, connection management and resource configuration management. These services can be reused by specific applications built on top of the middleware framework, such as multi-conferencing, video-on-demand etc.

CORBA (Common Object Request Broker Architecture) (CORBA) is a standard for middleware, defined by the Object Management Group (OMG), a consortium of more than seven hundred organisations including software industry leaders like Sun, HP, IBM, Microsoft and Rational. CORBA defines an environment for the distribution of interoperable objects across heterogeneous networks. The architecture has now reached a good level of maturity: the standard has existed for more than five years and is now implemented by more than ten commercial products.

CORBA makes it possible to generalize from three-tier architectures to fully distributed object architectures. An application is no longer composed of three layers, but every component can be distributed and can be seen at the same time as a client and as a server. Additionally, the OMG has defined a platform made of services that ease the integration of CORBA with traditional technologies (databases, transaction monitors etc.) and allow the development of CORBA industrial applications (transaction service, persistence service, event service, naming service, security service, concurrency service etc.).

DCOM (Distributed Component Object Model) (COM, 2000), also called COM+, is a CORBA-alternative middleware framework developed by Microsoft. DCOM is an extended version of Microsoft's Component Object Model (COM), and is the core part of the new Microsoft '.NET' initiative. The difference between COM and DCOM is that COM components run on a single machine, whereas DCOM components can be distributed across a network.

The main disadvantage of the DCOM framework is its limitation to Windows platforms. The main advantage is that Windows platforms offer a variety of tools for creating COM and DCOM components (Visual C++, Delphi, PowerBuilder etc.). Like CORBA, DCOM takes an object-oriented approach, with all applications referred to as objects with well defined interfaces. It is also important to note that the '.NET' initiative unifies server-side technologies (DCOM/COM+) with internet client access technologies such as Active Server Page (ASP) or ASP+.

The Java 2 Enterprise Edition (J2EE) provides an extensive environment for developing internet-based business or middleware frameworks. J2EE includes the Enterprise JavaBean technology for developing Java frameworks, and techniques like servlets and Java Server Pages (JSP) for internet browser access. More will be said about J2EE in the next Section, under server-side components.

Finally on frameworks (see the following Experience Note), it should be noted that designing a framework is a very demanding task that requires deep expertise both in OO design and in the target domain. It can only be undertaken after having designed several applications in the same domain. A prerequisite for designing a framework is a good vision of the technical and functional requirements of several applications in the domain. Defining architectural patterns for a domain constitutes the first step towards designing and implementing a framework.

Sodalia, an Italian company specializing in telecommunications software, has built for its own needs several network management frameworks. Their development process is split into reusable asset development (development *for* reuse) and application development (development *with* reuse). Reusable asset development consists of domain engineering and framework development. Domain engineering is the starting point for developing a business framework. It includes the following steps:

- business domain definition;
- requirements identification;
- object analysis;
- definition of domain architecture.

The resulting framework is an implementation of both the domain analysis and the domain architecture. One of the Telecom Network Management frameworks developed by Sodalia is made in C++ and based on CORBA for object distribution. The framework is aimed at network performance management. It is a very large system, with a size estimated at 10,000 function points. The framework has been instantiated several times to build turnkey systems for customers.

Its main variability points are functional and technical:

- type of network elements;
- communication protocol used for supervision;
- type of measures;
- scalability of the system (number of elements, number of users, volume of data etc.).

7.6 Component-Based Development

Component-based software development consists of assembling previously existing software components to build complex systems. Components are program units available in binary format. The component developer provides their well defined interface, but not the source code.

Components can range from small graphical user interface widgets to full-size applications such as word processors. They mainly differ from objects in that they are not general-purpose customisable classes, but highly specific ready-to-use plug-in components. Some application domains are already mature (GUI, business applications), in other words they are available on the market as commercial off-the-shelf (COTS) products.

More than any other reuse technique, component-based development makes it possible to draw a clear border between the development of reusable assets and their reuse. Indeed, if developing a reusable component remains a difficult task that demands good design and domain experience, the integration of the component into a new application becomes easier as a result of component assembly techniques.

Ideally, new applications are developed only by reusing existing components. Like horizontal frameworks, the developer has to provide the high-level design of the application and to write the main function that defines the control flow and information flow between the components. In contrast to the service objects provided by a horizontal framework, components are not necessarily designed to communicate and collaborate. They are not supposed to 'know each other' (principle of minimum coupling). The developer has to provide the integration architecture of the application, while the design and implementation of each component is already fixed.

In some cases a framework provides the integration structure for a set of components. This corresponds to the black-box approach to framework customization. The integration process can be partially automated, by means of tools that automatically select and retrieve components from a repository and match their specifications.

The integration framework (*Fig. 7.5*) has two main functions: it provides technical services to be used by components (avoiding the component developer's need to worry about low-level implementation details, and allowing him to focus on business logic); and it standardises the communication between components, enabling them to communicate without each knowing the internal aspects of the other. These two conditions are absolute prerequisites for having a system built on components that can be exchanged and reused in different contexts.

From the component developer's viewpoint, domain analysis is the most critical phase. In order to be broadly reusable, individual components have

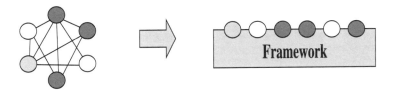

Fig. 7.5 Component integration through frameworks.

to be written to meet the requirements of a variety of applications in a specific domain. The current trend is toward a 'product line' approach: the developer designs and implements a complete set of components for a family of similar applications.

From the application developer's viewpoint, the user requirements specification should be made by having in mind which components are already available. According to Boehm (Boehm, 1995), 'in the old process, system requirements drove capabilities. In the new process, capabilities will drive system requirements . . . it is not a requirement if you can't afford it'. In the early stages of an application development (see the asset usage process defined in Section 4.1), the designer has to take into consideration which components are available, what integration effort they require, and whether to reuse them as they are or to build new components from scratch.

The component approach improves software development by reducing the amount of code that has to be written by the application designer. In particular, assembling previously existing components greatly reduces the time needed to test new applications. When a component is used in a large number of systems by different developers, knowledge about the component's usage, robustness and efficiency is available throughout the community of developers. The more a component is used the less it costs.

Component development is a powerful reuse technique. Its weakness lies in the technical and management skills required in a project team for component integration. The designer should rely on the available documentation of the components to be integrated as an unique source of information for understanding their behaviour and properties.

Components have to be used as they are: no adaptation, otherwise no advantages. Buying a component instead of developing it from scratch also creates a dependency of the user on the component provider. Components available on the market undergo frequent upgrading in response to error reports. Replacing an old component with its new version usually requires rewriting part of the integrating code and probably replacing other components which are not compatible with the new one.

7.6.1 Client-Side Components

Client-side components are software components that implement part of the presentation design and logic layers. They are assembled to build the client part of an application, visible to the end-user. They are generally made of basic GUI components provided by GUI toolkits (text fields, list boxes, buttons etc.). For example, a component aimed at capturing a user's address would be made of several text fields to enter the street name and city and a list box to select the country. Such a component can be reused by integrating it in a form.

Two alternative technologies for the development of client-side component-based applications are available on the market (Yourdon, 1997): ActiveX (ActiveX 1998; COM, 2000) and Java Beans (Java Beans, 2000).

ActiveX is the Microsoft solution for components. Initially, Microsoft proposed OLE (Object Linking and Embedding), which was an environment for component development and execution on a desktop. Such components are supported by a lot of development tools in the MS Windows environment, which are very simple to use but quite complex to develop.

Java Beans is the standard for building client-side components in Java. Java Beans are compatible with CORBA and ActiveX. Development tools make it possible to build applications by the graphical assembling of beans. ActiveX components and Java Beans are competing approaches to client-side component-based development. Compared to ActiveX, Java Beans are less mature but easier to develop. All major software industry leaders (except Microsoft) and the OMG have adopted Java Beans as the standard for client-side component development.

Fig. 7.6 shows a Java Beans assembling environment. The assembling is done graphically by selecting components ('beans') in the list, dragging and dropping them into the main area (representing the application being created). It is then possible to personalize their behavior by specifying their properties ('properties' window). It is often useful to aggregate several beans to build a more elaborate component. In this example, an invoice includes three text beans (to enter a number, a client and a date), a list of items, and two buttons (to add or remove items). Another bean is used to enter an item (including an article, a quantity and a price). In such an environment, it is not only possible to assemble beans in a static way (in order to build the presentation design layer) but also to specify the presentation logic layer (that is the interaction between components: the 'glue'). The links make it possible to specify that, in this example, pushing the 'add invoice item' button will activate the 'add item' bean, and that the values entered in the invoice number, client and date fields will be used to update corresponding attributes of the 'invoice' business object.

As this example shows, component technologies make it really possible to differentiate component development (like developing an 'invoice' Java Bean) from developing applications (like developing an accounting application by assembling Java Beans). Component development remains a demanding task, but application development can be much simplified by component assembly techniques (in this example, available GUI components appear in the 'beans list' on the right). Ideally, a new application could

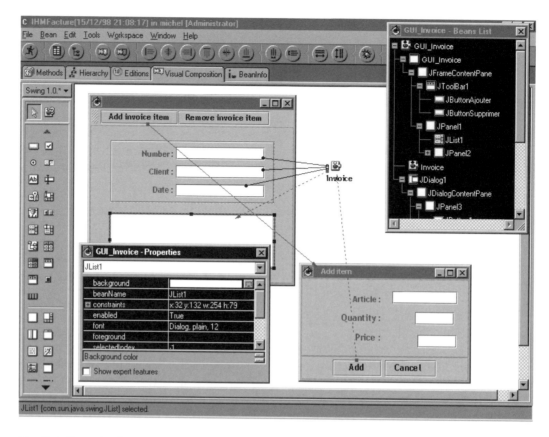

Fig. 7.6 Example of graphical environment to build and integrate client-side components (Java Beans).

be built just by assembling existing components. The application developer, however, has first to define the application architecture. This will drive the types of components to be considered and the way to assemble them. The application logic (the 'glue' between components) defines the control flow of the application and the way components interact. This is not defined by the components themselves, otherwise it would reduce their reusability by introducing too much coupling, too many dependencies.

A good component has to do as many useful things as possible, with as few assumptions as possible about what is around it. Such is the art of designing reusable components!

7.6.2 Server-Side Components

Server-side components are business objects implemented as components running on the business layer. Such a component implements the structure and behavior of one or several basic business entities (like an invoice) or higher level business processes (like invoicing) that involve several other components (such as invoice, client or purchase order). Server-side components are 'called' or used by the presentation layer to invoke business services and display business information. *Fig. 7.6* shows an example of some graphical components calling services of an 'invoice' business component.

Enterprise JavaBean (EJB) is the major technology used to implement server-side components. EJB (EJB) is based on Java and is the core of the J2EE (Java 2 Enterprise Edition) standard defined by Sun, but it is a completely different technology from JavaBeans. JavaBeans are graphical Java components, whereas EJBs are business transactional components, intended to be portable accross middleware. It is worthwhile to note that, besides EJB, J2EE also include technologies like JSP (Java Server Pages), useful for accessing back-end systems (and in particular EJBs) from a web application. EJB is not a product, but rather the specification of the interfaces between server-side Java components and the so-called application servers (the middleware that runs EJB on the server and provides distribution, transaction and security services). Such a concept makes it possible to obtain components that are reusable not only across operating systems but also across different vendors' middleware and databases. Although this standard is a Sun initiative, major software vendors (most of them in the middleware market) collaborate in using this specification, and provide implementations (commercial application server products): IBM, Netscape, BEA, Oracle, Fujitsu, Sybase, etc.

In the case of server-side components, the integration framework introduced at the beginning of this Section (*Fig. 7.5*) plays a particularly important role. Establishing a standardized interface between components (EJBs) and their framework (also called in this case 'application server' or 'container') brings several advantages when building and reusing components. The component developer focuses on business logic only. System-level programming is provided by the application server. Transaction management, directory (naming and identifying components at run-time), security, persistence and database access, as well as other technical services useful on a server (like life-cycle, multi-threading, load balancing etc.) are automatically managed for the EJB component by the application server. Moreover, the technical behaviour of components is declaratively customized. Features like transactional behavior, security features, creation and deletion behavior etc., can be specified by setting some component's properties.

EJBs are not the unique alternative for server-side components. Thanks to MTS (Microsoft Transaction Server) and DCOM/COM+ (COM, 2000), ActiveX can be considered as providing both client-side and server-side components. COM+ and MTS provide distribution and transaction manage-ment services necessary for implementing any business layer. ActiveX and COM+ are competing against EJBs and application servers, but are limited to the Microsoft world.

It is also worthwhile to note that the OMG is building a new component standard, based on CORBA. CCM, CORBA Component Model (CCM, 2000), is not a competitor of EJB, but is more general in the sense that it is not aimed at being limited to Java as the platform and programming language. EJB and CCM are complementary, because EJB recognizes that CORBA is a good platform on which to build an application server, and CCM has chosen EJB as its standard for Java components. In other words, a CORBA component implemented in Java is an EJB. Then, we can consider CCM as an extension of EJB, based on CORBA middleware but targeted to several languages.

In order to synthesize our vision of client and server components, let's compare the main features of both families of technologies (the Microsoft family with DCOM/COM+, MTS and ActiveX, and the Java family with EJB and JavaBeans). Table 7.1 refers to the eight technical characteristics of a component defined in Chapter 2 (see Section 2.2 for more details).

- Interoperability: two components should be able to communicate even if they run on different machines and are implemented with different languages.

- Portability: across platforms, operating systems, databases or GUI envi-ronments.

- Differentiation of interface and implementation: differentiating a compo-nent's usage from its implementation.

- Composition: components can be aggregated into larger-grained compo-nents.

- Self-descriptiveness: the user of a component can discover its interface dynamically.

- Location transparency: components interact independently of the phys-ical nodes where they are located.

- Security: control the component's origin and control its access to local resources. The component is also able to control the access to its own services (access right management at the level of each component).

- Plug and play: run-time portability.

Table 7.1 Component technologies comparison.

	.NET / DCOM / MTS / ActiveX	J2EE / EJB / JavaBeans
General features		
Client-side	YES ActiveX can be graphical components. ASPs allow components on the web server.	YES Java Beans are graphical components implemented in Java. JSPs allow components on the Web server.
Server-side	YES But DCOM and MTS provide stateless servers (they do not remember previous requests).	YES EJBs are server-side business components implemented in Java. EJBs can be stateless or stateful.
Services	DCOM and MTS provide distribution, directory and transaction management on Windows servers.	Application servers provide standardized services for distribution, directory, transactions, persistence, concurrency, security, fault-tolerance and load-balancing.
Building components	Can be implemented in Visual Basic, C++ or other languages such as Delphi. Developing server-side components can become complex (C++ APIs).	Traditional Java programming. Java Beans are easy to create. Actually all Java graphical objects are Beans. EJBs require architectural design skills (for instance distinction between 'entity' and 'session' beans).
Reusing components	ActiveX is easy to reuse on the client side and is supported by many graphical development tools.	Easy assembly of JavaBeans. EJBs are easily assembled and deployed thanks to specific development environments. The standardization ensures minimal lock-in to a particular vendor.
Technical criteria		
Interoperability	MEDIUM Supported by many development tools but mostly on Windows.	YES Interoperability with many tools and platforms, and with CORBA and ActiveX.
Portability	NO Mostly Windows NT and Windows 2000.	YES Independence from OS (ensured by Java), databases, and application servers (ensured by EJB standard). Requires Java as the programming language.
Differentiation of interface and implementation	YES Thanks to an Interface Definition Language (IDL).	YES This is native in Java.

Table 7.1 continued

	.NET / DCOM / MTS / ActiveX	J2EE / EJB / JavaBeans
Composition	YES	YES
Self-descriptiveness	YES Interfaces are declared in a registry.	YES Introspection mechanism: no need of interface repository.
Location transparency	YES Thanks to DCOM.	YES Thanks to RMI (Remote Method Invocation), CORBA, DCOM.
Security	MEDIUM Digital signature; but the access to local resources is not fully controlled.	YES Beans are executed in a 'sand box' that protects local resources.
Plug and play	NO Objects are compiled to run in a given environment.	YES Provided by Java.

7.6.3 Internet Components

As described in Section 7.2 internet components are graphical components assembled in a web page, generally as part of a horizontal or vertical portal. For this reason, these components are sometimes called 'portlets', but also 'channels', 'gadgets' or 'e-clips', depending on the technologies and vendors. Main portal vendors include Plumtree, Hummingbird, Hyperwave, Autonomy and Opentext for horizontal portals, and BEA, Brodvision and Vignette for vertical portals.

Such components may have different purposes:

- display HTML information taken from different formats;

- simple applications, very common on the internet (forums, chat, e-mail boxes, etc.);

- connect to enterprise systems (ERPs, business intelligence, knowledge management, etc.);

- display contents from external sources (public web sites or partners' extranets).

This last option corresponds to what is called content syndication. Because of their modularity and easy integration into web pages, internet components are very reusable by nature. They can be developed in HTML, XML, JavaScript, ASP or JSP. However, there is no standard for developing them and integrating them into a portal. For this reason, internet components can be reused in the same portal environment only. However, some vendors have set up user communities and common marketplaces for sharing and exchanging components (Gadget; Tracks). In this case, the vendor produces components to be sold or given free to customers, but also qualifies third-party components developed by user community members. Once the component is validated, the vendor commits to its distribution and maintenance.

7.6.4 From Component Reuse to Information Reuse

Since internet components are used to access, process and display information in a standard format (HTML or XML), but are reusable only within a proprietary environment, an alternative is to reuse the information itself. Content syndication is an emerging technique which is gaining more and more importance on the internet. Publishing data across web sites (as opposed to publishing data from a web site to end users) is becoming a fundamental requirement for B2B systems. However reusing, sharing and distributing information between different companies' web sites requires the solution of two problems.

1. All parties need a common vocabulary. Several efforts in this direction have started with the development of XML and the definition of domain-specific DTDs (document type definitions) (XML). XML allows the sharing of information in a simple and standard format. For the publisher and the subscriber to be able to share a common understanding, a DTD (ensuring common interpretation of the data) must be specified. In other words, a DTD gives a meaning to an XML document, beyond its syntax. See for example (Ontology 2000) (ontologies are also addressed in the agent-based system Section of this Chapter).

2. There needs to be an agreement on the protocol used to exchange data between web sites (as opposed to HTTP, the protocol used to publish data to the end-user's browser). The World Wide Web Consortium (W3C) is working on the ICE (Information and Content Exchange) protocol, proposed by a group of companies led by Vignette, Adobe and Sun.

ICE (ICE, 1998; ICE, 2001) defines a standard solution for server-to-server syndication, in order to distribute and aggregate content between heterogenous servers. This is necessary for consumer portals (for instance syndication of news articles concerning industry, sport, entertainment etc. to a unique portal) as well as for enterprise portals and B2B portals (for instance a company publishing its updated catalogue to its distributors). ICE defines the protocol for publishing information to a web site. Most aspects of the standard are not included in a client protocol like HTTP. The main features of ICE include: schedule for publication and updates, security, personalisation, delivery (direct to a web site or to an agreed intermediate location), and approval process (in order to keep control of what is published on one's web site). It is now even possible to use such syndication techniques to publish and share internet components among a community.

7.7 Agent-Based Systems

Recently the concept of *software agents* has been proposed as an extension of the object model. Agents are integrated systems that (1) internally incorporate major capabilities drawn from several areas (artificial intelligence, databases, programming languages, theory of computing) and (2) externally communicate with other agents through a communication language which is independent of the specific structural features of individual agents.

From the agent viewpoint, most complex software systems and applications are conceived as organizations of cooperative agents. Basically, the notion of software agents provides a natural metaphor for modelling system components and their interactions: a survey (CACM, 1994) is available. Software agents enhance software reusability at least for the two following reasons.

- In contrast to objects, agents allow software integration not only at a syntactic level (where system components commonly agree on a set of data structure definitions and on the meaning of the operations on those structures), but also at a semantic level: system components communicate in terms of knowledge transfer instead of data transfer. Knowledge interchange is achieved through the use of a standard knowledge representation language.

- Agents' behaviour is usually highly customisable to new operational conditions and new interaction protocols. In fact, artificial intelligence and database research provides a number of techniques and mechanisms for learning and system adaptability.

From the application developer viewpoint, high-level design is the more intensive phase. The designer has to identify the role and responsibility of each agent in the organization and define their mutual interactions. In

150

contrast to component-based development, the designer has a high degree of freedom in the customisation of the behaviour of each agent. In contrast to application frameworks, agents offer a *grey-box* approach to customisation, where the source code of the agents is not modified but the internal resources and reasoning capabilities are specified through a declarative script language.

Agents have great promise for enhancing flexibility in the patterns of interactions between the components of an application, and for improving the reusability of single agents and of the application design. Software agents are particularly advantageous for the development of heterogeneous distributed systems.

Agents may be implemented using different programming languages and for different computing platforms. Agents can interoperate because they share the same communication language and a common vocabulary, which contains words that are appropriate to common application areas and whose meanings are described in terms of shared ontologies.

Unfortunately, agent development today resembles more an art form than a branch of engineering: most of the research and development of software agents is based on proprietary design architectures invented from scratch each time. For agent technology to move out of the laboratories and become a viable solution for industrial applications, it must recognize the fundamental importance of software engineering principles for managing the development complexity of large-scale systems. The most promising approach is the development of agent-based application frameworks. A few examples already exist (see Sycara, 1996).

7.8 Comparison of Techniques

In this Section we review all the reuse techniques described in the previous Sections in terms of their differences and similarities. In particular we compare the techniques from the application developer's viewpoint (developing *with* reuse) and from the reusable asset developer's viewpoint (developing *for* reuse). We also set out the strengths and weaknesses of each technique.

7.8.1 Developing WITH Reuse: Which Types of Artefacts Are Reused?

Traditional object-oriented technology, component development and software agents mainly promote reuse of code and associated design models.

The developer retrieves reusable pieces of code and models from repositories and integrates them into more complex systems. Components can offer complex domain-dependent functionality, but they have to be reused as they are and without change (black-box reuse). Customization is necessary for more flexibility, but is generally limited. Software agents are extremely flexible and adaptable, but usually do not support fine-grain reuse since they require considerable computational resources.

Software architectures and design patterns document design solutions that are proven by experience to be effective. They allow the reuse of structural relationships between the software artefacts of an application, not of the artefact itself. Architectures are usually general-purpose, while design patterns may be organized in pattern languages for specific application domains. Frameworks support reuse of architecture, design and code. They are semi-complete applications that can generate by customisation a family of specific applications for the same domain. For this reason, they constitute the most advanced form of reuse.

Finally, we saw that internet architectures and the standardization of content in HTML and XML are generating a shift, away from the reuse of software artefacts toward the reuse of content (information), and away from the integration of back-end components toward integration of internet components on the web page.

7.8.2 Developing FOR Reuse: Which Phase of the Software Life Cycle Does the Technique Involve?

Developing components and frameworks for a specific application domain requires a careful analysis of the domain, in order to recognize the stable entities and relationships that can be captured by reusable assets. In addition, component development requires an economic analysis of the market in which the components will be sold (internally within a company, or externally). Identifying reusable design patterns also requires long experience in developing families of similar applications for the same domain.

Software architectures and application frameworks mainly deal with high-level design aspects. They differ in that software architectures are general-purpose and formally specified, while frameworks can be domain-dependent and informally documented. Frameworks generally include several design patterns that are applied to different parts as basic design principles.

Components and software agents are developed to solve the difficult design

Table 7.2 Comparison of techniques.

	Strength	Weakness
OOT	Provides basic reuse enablers like modularity, information hiding, aggregation and specialization.	Requires significant modelling effort. Usage of OOT does not guarantee reuse.
Design patterns	Facilitate retrieval of design solutions, provide guidelines for the development process, improve communication among designers.	Implementation from scratch.
Frameworks	Reuse of object model (design, code) plus architecture.	Framework development requires high domain expertise and deep understanding of object design. Usage of a framework imposes an architecture.
Components	Development of external markets. Easy to integrate.	Less customizable.
Software agents	Highly customizable and adaptable, allow easy reconfiguration of complex systems.	Not yet mature and consolidated technology.

problems that can characterize an application and that usually are described as design patterns. Application frameworks can support both (1) the development of components and software agents and (2) their integration to build complex systems.

Object-oriented class libraries, application frameworks, components and software agents require extensive coding and testing before they can be released for reuse.

References

1. Abowd, G., Allen, R. and Garlan D. (1993) Using Style to Give Meaning to Software Architecture. In *Proc. Of SIGSOFT '93: Foundations of Software Engineering*, Software Engineering Notes, (Dec. 1993). 118(3), pp. 9–20.
2. ActiveX (1998) *Magic: An ActiveX Control and DCOM Sample Using ATL.* http://www.microsoft.com/com/wpaper/default.asp#ActiveXpapers
3. Boehm, B. (1995) Proc. SEI/MCC Symposium on the Use of COTS in System Integration.

4. Brown, A.W. Carney, D.J. McFalls M.D (eds), SEI Special Report CMU/SEI-95-SR-007, Software Engineering Institute, Pittsburgh PA, 1995.

5. Booch, G. (1991) *Object-Oriented Analysis and Design with Applications.* Benjamin/Cummings Publishing Company Inc., Redwood City, CA.

6. Brugali, D., Menga, G. and Aarsten, A. (1997) The Framework Life Span. In *Communications of the ACM*, October 1997.

7. Buschmann, F., Meunier, R., Rohner, H., Sommerlad, P. and Stal, M. (1996) *A System of Patterns: Pattern-Oriented Software Architecture.* John Wiley & Sons; West Sussex.

8. CACM (1994) Special Issue on Intelligent Agents, *Communications of the ACM*, Vol. 37, No. 7, July 1994.

9. CACM (1996) Special Issue on Design Patterns, *Communications of the ACM*, Vol. 39, No. 10, October 1996.

10. CACM (1997) Special Issue on Object-Oriented Application Frameworks, *Communications of the ACM*, Vol. 40 No. 10, October 1997.

11. CCM (2000http://www.omg.org/technology/documents/recent/corba_iiop.htm and http://cgi.omg.org/cgi-bin/doc?omg/00–06–01.pdf

12. CetusLinks http://www.mini.net/cetus/software.html

13. COM (2000) DCOM Architecture, Microsoft Corporation. http://www.microsoft.com/com/

14. CORBA: http://www.omg.org

15. Dosher, D. and Hodges, R. (1997) Sematech's Experiences with the CIM Framework. In *Communications of the ACM*, Vol. 40, No. 10, October 1997.

16. EJB: http://java.sun.com/products/ejb

17. Fowler, M. (1997) *Analysis Patterns.* Addison-Wesley.

18. Gadget: http://gadget.plumtree.com

19. Gamma, E., Helm, R., Johnson, R. and Vlissides, J. (1995) *Design Patterns: Elements of Reusable Object-Oriented Software.* Addison-Wesley.

20. ICE (1998) http://www.w3.org

21. ICE (2001) http://www.icestandard.org

22. JavaBeans (2000) http://www.javasoft.com/beans/

23. Larman, C. (1998) *Applying UML and Patterns – An Introduction to OO Analysis and Design.* Prentice-Hall.

24. Ontology (2000) http://www.ontology.org

25 Powell, D. and Miller, T. (1997) Using Delphi 3, Special Edition, *Computer Literacy.*

26. Rumbaugh, J., Blaha, M., Premerlani, W., Eddy, F. and Lornsen, W. (1991) *Object-Oriented Modeling and Design.* Prentice-Hall International Editions.

27. Sycara, K., Pannu, A., Williamson, M. and Zeng, D. (1996) Distributed Intelligent Agents. In *IEEE Expert, Special Issue on Intelligent Systems and their Applications*, Vol. 11, No. 6, Dec. 1996, pp. 36–46.

28. Lengdell, M. (1995) TINA Resource Architecture Overview. Document EN_M.L.001_1.1_95, TINA Consortium, April 1995.

29. Tracks: http://tracks.hyperwave.com

30. UML: http://www.omg.org/technology/uml/index.htm

31. XML : http://www.xml.com

32. Yourdon, E. (1997) CORBA/Java vs DCOM/ActiveX. *Application Development Strategies*, Vol. IX, No. 6, June 1997.

Two Major Case Histories

8

ABSTRACT

Among the projects we have interviewed while preparing this book, we have chosen to develop a detailed comparison of four of them. This Chapter presents a description of two of the most significant reuse experiences in Europe. Sodalia (Italy) and Thomson-CSF (France) appear to be very successful: reuse is well integrated into their software processes (and to a certain extent to their company cultures) and helped significantly to improve their product offerings. They present interesting similarities and differences, both in their business context and in their approach to reuse. The two cases are presented in parallel.

Sodalia

Thomson-CSF

Company

Sodalia is a relatively young Italian SME (about six years old), specializing in software for telecommunications. It is a joint venture of two telecommunications operators: Telecom Italia and Bell Atlantic.

Thomson-CSF is a French multinational industrial group. The group is made up of several companies or business units, developing products and systems based on electronics and software.

Staff

Sodalia employs a staff of 300, all dedicated to software production.

Thomson-CSF has 50,000 employees. 5,000 are dedicated to software production.

Business Context

Sodalia's parent companies are its main, but not exclusive, customers. Sodalia's business consists in providing customized telecommunications software products such as Telecom Network Management Systems (TNM). The company has several product families. This means that each product in a family is adapted to each customer context. In particular in the field of TNM, different products offer different levels of services and different functions (such as network configuration management, performance management, fault management . . .).

The role of the Thomson-CSF business units is to sell hardware and software (civil and military) systems all over the world. Each business unit has its own business, such as:

- TT&S for training simulation systems;

- Thomson Airsys WSD for weapon system development;

- Thomson Airsys ATM for multi-domain control centres, like air traffic control centres;

- Syseca – Industrie & Tertiaire: a software provider in the industry and services sectors.

Sodalia

Thomson-CSF

Reuse Drivers and Expectations

- Improve software development productivity.

- Improve company competitiveness by anticipating and meeting market needs and trends.

- Develop the company's offerings and product lines.

Each business unit may have its own reuse expectation. In general, the objective is to improve the business unit competitiveness by developing flexible product lines and thus to achieve reductions in costs and time to market. Moreover product lines are a way to be closer to evolving market requirements.

Reuse Strategy

Sodalia's offerings comprise a set of product lines. Each product line addresses one or several well identified business domains (all within telecommunications). Sodalia has set up a domain engineering process, to define domain commonalities, clearly separated from application engineering. This strategy allows the development of several applications within a domain from a common domain model and from common domain requirements.

Applications are also developed from existing assets. Software assets may be vertical (specific to a product line) or horizontal (implementing common technical infrastructure features).

Several domains have been selected for reuse. For instance:

- test benches;

- small and large air traffic control centres;

- automatic train supervision for operational control centres;

- training systems;

- civil aircraft simulators.

For these domains, the strategy is to be able to build a new system easily from existing ones. This requires the ability to analyse commonalities and variabilities between customer requirements and existing product features.

Sodalia

Thomson-CSF

Reuse Introduction Steps

- Define reuse processes.

- Set up a reuse organization.

- Implement a tool to manage an asset repository.

- Provide support for tool and methodology.

- Undertake pilot projects to experiment with reuse and related technologies.

- Promote reuse to the staff.

- Generalize reuse processes to all projects.

Sodalia has completed all these steps and is now improving reuse practices and setting up processes and metrics to measure reuse efficiency and improvements. All projects are concerned with reuse, and a culture of reuse has spread to all staff.

At corporate level, the reuse leader promotes, supports and coordinates reuse and its progressive adoption by different business units.

At business unit level a reuse correspondent within the business unit drives the introduction of reuse.

1. Initialization of the reuse program:
   - formalize business objectives;
   - obtain management commitment;
   - define process model.

2. Assessment of business units:
   - domain assessment (to evaluate the reuse potential of a domain);
   - reuse capability assessment (to evaluate business units' readiness to start a reuse program).

3. Definition of the reuse plan:
   - define reuse strategic plan;
   - prepare economic model.

4. Execution and improvement:
   - incremental implementation of reuse plan;
   - reuse tracking and reporting (every three months);
   - improvement plan.

Five Thomson-CSF business units had reached step 4 at the time of this study. The reuse leader is continuously introducing reuse into new business units or new domains. Several other business units have recently asked to be part of the reuse program.

Sodalia   Thomson-CSF

Software Process Maturity

Process maturity is quite high. The company is ISO 9001 certified. It has a strong quality team (separate from the reuse team). The company has reached CMM level 3.

It varies from one business unit to another, but most of the business units involved in the reuse program have now reached a good level of maturity: they are all ISO 9001 certified, their process model is driven by the DoD 2167A standard, and they have reached CMM level 2 or 3. However, most of the business units involved in reuse were at level 1 when reuse was introduced. The CMM level grew together with the reuse level.

Management

Sodalia management is strongly committed to reuse. Software is the only business of the company and the reuse programme is a very important part of the corporate strategy. The management board has dedicated very significant resources to the reuse programme. It is systematically informed of reuse activities and results.

Top management, at corporate level, is convinced of the necessity of reuse. Reuse has been chosen as a key improvement priority by the software Common Efficiency Team (CET). CETs are transverse teams, defining corporate strategy and proposing improvements.

Reuse Co-ordination and Tracking

A reuse leader is in charge of the co-ordination and tracking of all reuse activities. The reuse leader is in charge of managing the reuse team (assets, repository, support to projects) and the reuse processes. She must co-ordinate reuse activities according to project schedules, and define priorities (in terms of asset development) according to

Reuse is managed at corporate level. A specific unit (Thomson-CSF Technologies et Méthodes) is responsible for:

- promoting and disseminating reuse culture into the whole group;

- monitoring reuse adoption in all business units;

Sodalia

Thomson-CSF

Reuse Co-ordination and Tracking (continued)

company strategy (business priorities). The reuse leader periodically reports reuse accomplishment and expenditure to management. Metrics and an economic model are currently being introduced. Costs can be easily recorded since reuse activities are mainly concentrated in the reuse team.

- co-ordinating reuse activities throughout the group;

- tracking and consolidating reuse results from all business units.

For this purpose, Thomson-CSF uses a complex economic model defined by the SPC (see Chapter 4 on processes for more information on the Software Productivity Consortium).

Co-ordination and monitoring meetings are periodically scheduled between the reuse leader and every business unit involved in the reuse program.

Reuse Organization

The reuse leader is at the head of a reuse group (10 people out of 200 software engineers). This group is responsible for the following tasks.

- Reuse process definition and update.

- Methodological support to projects.

- Participation in the development of reusable assets.

- Asset qualification.

- Asset management and maintenance.

- External asset acquisition.

The reuse programme is driven in a centralized way by the reuse leader. He is responsible for reuse promotion, support during reuse adoption, reuse co-ordination, and tracking and reporting consolidated reuse results.

However, business units remain independent profit centres. Each of them is free to 'subscribe' to the reuse program or not, and if it does, to use its own technologies, approach and repository. No software is shared at corporate level among different business units. Each business unit has its own reuse program, reuse organization and software assets.

Sodalia | Thomson-CSF

Reuse Organization (continued)

- Development and maintenance of an in-house tool to manage the asset repository.

- Management of the repository.

- Reuse co-ordination.

- Reuse tracking and reporting.

The reuse team supports all reuse activities. In particular, it provides substantial help to projects for reusable asset identification, development and validation. In consequence, reuse is not considered as a constraint for applications projects (they generally don't have a significant overhead because of reuse) but as a help (they benefit from existing assets and methodological support).

Sometimes a member of the reuse team is temporarily integrated into a project development team with the objective of developing a reusable asset.

Business units involved in reuse have, at least, a reuse correspondent in charge of driving the reuse program within the business unit and reporting to corporate level.

Reuse Roles

Reuse leader.

Reuse support engineer.

Reusable assets developer.

Reusable assets repository manager.

Reuse leader (corporate level).

Reuse correspondent (in each business unit).

Configuration manager (not restricted to reuse).

Sodalia

Thomson-CSF

Human Aspects

The software staff is relatively young, with a good educational level and a strong background in object modelling and object technologies. Moreover, reuse has been a part of the company culture from an early stage. Thus it is naturally accepted by a majority of the software staff. No rewards policy has been necessary. Reuse news and results are periodically communicated to the staff, and every software engineer has direct access to the reuse repository and to on-line reuse and quality procedures. Software engineers are generally trained in reuse techniques.

Software engineers are generally well experienced in the domain and technologies they are working on.

Most of them are trained in reuse. Moreover reuse introduction presentations are made to managers and staff.

No rewards policy has been set up. Few roadblocks have been encountered in terms of human aspects because staff and processes are generally mature and experience has shown that the staff is not reluctant if management is strongly committed and if reuse is presented as strategic. Sometimes some engineers see reuse as a restriction of their creativity.

Processes

The impact of reuse on the software development process and on the quality process has been defined. Additional reuse-specific processes have been formalized and applied.

Domain engineering includes the following activities:

- domain definition and scoping;

- domain requirements definition;

- domain modelling;

- domain architecture definition.

Each business unit is responsible for its own processes for systems development, qualification, configuration management and assets repository management. Development processes are defined in the corporate quality system for each type of system (such as simulation, embedded, . . .). They are based on DoD 2167A.

Additionally, domain engineering and reuse management guidelines are defined at corporate level but instantiated and applied by each business unit.

Sodalia

Thomson-CSF

Processes (continued)

Such domain models are the starting point for developing an application. Sometimes such a model leads to a framework development.

Reusable assets are generally developed by the reuse team. Sometimes they are developed by the project team with support from the reuse team, in such a way that there is no extra effort for the project team to make assets reusable. Sometimes project and reuse teams have contradictory objectives (reusability vs delivery date).

The reuse team also centralises the acquisition of external assets (commercial or freeware) as well as their customization and support.

A specific process has been set up for the management of the reusable assets repository and its relationships with the configuration management policy.

Asset validation includes separate quality and reusability assessments.

The objective of domain engineering is to provide assets and also to define processes to use them. The activities are:

- domain management;

- domain definition;

- product family engineering (requirements, architecture, design, components implementation);

- process engineering (defining how to use the components);

- verification and validation.

Methods, Techniques and Technologies

Domain modelling and application modelling are performed using UML. Domain modelling implies a 'commonality and variability' analysis: every domain model element's variability through time and applications is studied.

Domain modelling is performed using a textual language (in order not to impose a new graphical formalism or tool on business units). Domain modelling implies a 'commonality and variability' analysis: every domain model element's variability

Sodalia	Thomson-CSF

Methods, Techniques and Technologies (continued)

Reusable assets are often class libraries or OO frameworks.

Development is undertaken in C++, from an OO design made with UML.

Advanced technologies and techniques like design patterns, distributed objects and CORBA are frequently used.

Technical class libraries are often used to implement technical architectures. For instance: bridge from C++ application to relational databases, LAN communication (socket libraries),

through time and applications is studied.

Application modelling is traditionally performed using SA/RT, SA/DT or OO modelling. The choice is up to each business unit or project. However all projects use a set of development tools, pre-determined at corporate level, called ATGL (Atelier Thomson de Génie Logiciel), and made of commercial CASE tools). OO techniques are far from being systematically applied.

Implementation is generally undertaken in C or Ada (and C++ for GUI).

Assets

Assets are designed to be reused. They are large grained (complete domain models, frameworks, libraries). They may be vertical (domain-specific) or horizontal (technical infrastructure). Assets generally contain code, models, analysis and design documentation, and test cases.

Example of vertical assets

A TMN framework for performance management. This framework implements the basic architecture of all performance management systems (made of data collection modules, database, reporting, data analysis, SNMP interface . . .). It is customizable from different points of view:

Assets are traditionally software elements (requirements documents, design documents, source code, test cases). Reusable assets are not packaged differently from other software pieces. All assets are vertical (domain-specific). Asset reusability is determined according to domain analysis results.

Example of vertical asset

A generic air traffic control application for small centres. From this asset, a new application is built by adding code corresponding to functions that are specific to this particular system (and possibly removing unwanted functions).

Sodalia   ## Thomson-CSF

Assets (continued)

- protocol used to communicate with network elements (GDMO, CMIP, SNMP, proprietary . . .);

- type of network elements (different network, different constructors);

- types of measures;

- scalability (number of elements, number of users, volume of data . . .).

The framework size is estimated as 10,000 function points.

Examples of horizontal assets

- A tracing library.

- A GUI objects library.

- A library to access application configuration files.

- An alarm browser (used in different telecommunications domains).

Repository

Sodalia's repository contains about 100 assets. These assets are extracted from their original applications and put into a centralized configuration management system (ClearCase) that is dedicated to reusable assets. The repository contains domain requirements and models, vertical assets (components and frameworks), and horizontal assets.

For each Thomson-CSF business unit, the repository consists of a 'product baseline' that, for a given domain or product line, contains the best compromise between commonalities and variabilities. This means that, for efficiency reasons, not all software assets corresponding to specific (and rare) cases should be kept in the baseline; on the other

Sodalia

Thomson-CSF

Repository (continued)

All developers have access to the corporate repository through an in-house tool, called SALMS (Sodalia Assets Library Management System). This tool has its own database where asset descriptions are stored together with 'pointers' to the assets themselves. SALMS offers functions to developers:

- multi-criteria asset search;

- asset visualization and evaluation;

- asset import from the repository;

and additional functions to the asset repository manager:

- access rights management;

- usage statistics;

- asset insertion and storage into the repository;

- asset update (with version management);

- definition of the classification scheme.

SALMS is interfaced with ClearCase in order to manage assets and asset descriptions in a consistent way and to be able to manage asset configuration and changes.

hand, the baseline must not be reduced to the minimal intersection between all product releases, because otherwise reuse opportunities may be missed (in the case of features that are common to two systems but not to all of them). All lifecycle work products are kept in the baseline (from requirements to test cases).

Each new product version is built by extracting useful software assets from the product baseline. Of course, this requires that the baseline is very well organized, and that changes are controlled. The baseline is periodically updated according to recent product releases and configurations are managed. Different business units may use different configuration management tools.

Sodalia

Thomson-CSF

Actual Reuse Results

For Sodalia, reuse allowed a better approach to the market and more flexible offerings.

The common repository contains about a hundred large-grained valuable assets that capture business and technical expertise.

Existing assets have been used between one and five times.

The reuse policy is considered as very positive and fruitful by the management. Costs are controlled because there is an established budget for the reuse team. But there are not any quantitative results about process efficiency, economic benefits or return on investment because the necessary measurements have not been set up yet.

Though reuse is promoted and driven at corporate level, each business unit is a different and independent company. Thus, the objective is not to share software across business units, and each of them performs reuse in a different context, with different constraints and different market opportunities.

Some business units have not had a sufficient level of experience in the relevant domains, or sufficient business opportunities to capitalize on a selected business domain by reusing.

Others have achieved very positive results (we only deal with results that are clearly attributable to reuse).

- For one business unit, average time to market has been reduced from two years (in 1993) to eleven months (in 1997).

- Significant productivity improvements have made it possible to reduce costs, and thus to become more competitive.

- The reuse level (percentage of reused code within a new system) can go higher than 75 per cent when product lines are well mastered.

The reuse improvement process objective is not only to increase the

Sodalia   Thomson-CSF

Actual Reuse Results (continued)

reuse level, but also to decrease the cost of reusing software. This cost (called reuse relative cost) is computed by comparing the cost of reusing a line of code to the cost of producing it. The general trend shows that when the reuse level increases, the reuse relative cost decreases. This can be explained by the fact that both indicators reveal reuse maturity: generally the more software a project reuses, the more efficient the reuse process is.

Regarding return on investment, Thomson-CSF found that assets must be used three times to break even.

In general, business units involved in the reuse programme have increased their market shares over two years. Reuse is definitely seen as a key factor in achieving this result.

Conclusion

It is interesting to recapitulate some of the main similarities and differences.

Similarities

- Although they are in different business sectors, both companies have a product line approach and have the same expectations concerning reuse: improve competitiveness by strengthening their offerings.

- Both approaches are based on domain engineering.

- Both companies have an official reuse programme, considered as strategic, to which the management is strongly committed.

- Both companies have a good level of software process maturity (probably above the average).

- For both companies reuse is largely managed in a centralized way by a single reuse leader.

Differences

- Company sizes are very different. Thomson-CSF is very large and consists of independent business units, so that reuse cannot be applied in a completely uniform way. Reuse is coordinated at corporate level but practised independently in each business unit. By contrast, Sodalia actually shares assets at corporate level.

- Sodalia deliberately employs new technologies (OO, UML, CORBA, frameworks . . .) whereas Thomson-CSF uses them occasionally.

- Sodalia has a full reuse-oriented organization (reuse tasks and overheads are handled by a dedicated team, independent from projects), whereas the Thomson-CSF business units are structured by business domains (within a domain, the same engineers manage the product baseline and develop systems). In Sodalia's case reuse roles are specialized whereas this is not the case for Thomson-CSF business units.

- Sodalia has not yet implemented a measurement programme whereas Thomson-CSF measures reuse processes and reuse costs and benefits. However Sodalia's reuse organization allows more effective control of reuse costs.

Two Smaller Case Histories

9

ABSTRACT

This Chapter presents a description of successful reuse as experienced in two smaller European companies – ELIOP (Spain) and Chase Computer Services (UK). As in the previous Chapter the two cases are presented in parallel.

Eliop

Chase

Company

ELIOP SA is a Spanish company. Its main activity is the delivery of industrial control systems.

Chase Computer Services is a small UK company. It delivers systems for clients in the mutual marine insurance industry.

Staff

ELIOP has about 100 employees, 30 of them directly involved in software development.

Chase has 27 employees, most of whom are directly involved in software development.

Business Context

ELIOP develops systems for applications such as remote telecontrol, process automation and energy management. The systems are of two main types: microprocessor-based in-house manufactured equipment with embedded software, and software running on standard computers. They often control critical industrial processes, and require real-time continuous operation. Software is a very important part of the added value of ELIOP products.

The requirements of Chase's customers, while broadly similar, differ in detail. Their specific needs are met by customizing from a standard product line. The company is undergoing a period of rapid change: the size of projects is growing, and the company is converting its platform technology to client-server.

Reuse Drivers and Expectations

- Encourage better practice. Reusable assets must be of high quality, thus demanding better methods and tools in all part of the development process.

- Reduce development time, especially for coding and testing.

- Increase reliability, by using well-tested reusable modules.

Chase's aim was to improve software development practices by introducing software reuse, making it possible to capitalize on the similarities between the requirements of different clients.

Specific goals were as follows.

- Enhance the quality and maintainability of applications.

172

| Eliop | Chase |

Reuse Drivers and Expectations (continued)

- Reduce cost. While the effort of producing reusable assets is higher than for normal assets, their use saves other development costs. An estimated reduction of 30 per cent in development costs was expected, with further savings in maintenance. This figure did not take account of investment costs, and should be considered only as a measure of broad expectation.

- Increase customer satisfaction. A large improvement in customer satisfaction was envisaged, though no quantitative objectives were stated.

- Increase the efficiency, effectiveness and productivity of the development process.

- Improve the company's ability to meet the needs of its customers, and thus achieve competitive advantage.

Reuse Strategy

Prior to the introduction of reuse, software practice followed the classical life-cycle. New projects were often treated as upgrades to previous software, by means of additions and modifications. The following early strategic decisions were made.

- Since a permanent problem is limited human resources, reuse must satisfy two conditions: the extra work of developing reusable assets must be limited, and return on investment must be obtained quickly.

- Reuse was already practised, but not in a systematic or organized

It was judged to be of prime importance that reuse should be considered in a much wider context than the usual, narrow, technological viewpoint of just reusing code. In other words, reuse should be pervasive throughout the development process.

It was recognized that any process improvement has to be a balance between the effort needed to achieve the improvement and the imperative of carrying on normal business – between putting the business at risk by experimenting with business-critical projects and getting no benefit through addressing non-critical

173

| **Eliop** | **Chase** |

Reuse Strategy (continued)

way. The objective therefore became to introduce systematic reuse.

- Only horizontal reuse had previously been practised, with no recognition of the concept of vertical reuse. The focus was shifted to vertical reuse, because (a) company's products lie in a small number of domains, (b) it allows reuse of high-level and application-specific software, while horizontal reuse is normally restricted to lower layers of products.

- White-box reuse was adopted because it entails less cost and risk. It is also organizationally simpler, because specific people need not be assigned to develop and maintain reusable assets.

- Reuse was to be extended from source code to many other asset types, including specifications, designs, test procedures, and other documents. Assets were to be standardized, based on the application of coding rules for source code and templates for documents.

- Sustained management support was recognized as critical, because reuse is a long-term investment.

processes. In a company of Chase's size, selecting a non-business-critical project to be an experimental guinea pig for reuse would be very difficult, so getting the right balance was a serious challenge.

Eliop | Chase

Reuse Introduction Steps

- Determine reuse approach, based on available knowledge about reuse.

- Review current process, to identify and evaluate factors influencing reuse, and to discuss and select ideas for improvement. This was done by meetings, each addressing a process area. Effort ~ 150 hours.

- Define process improvement goals.

- Identify and set up appropriate metrics. The **ami** method was used: it is a method to derive metrics from a set of goals defined by the organization.

- Select and install necessary tools.

- Train staff in new process, methods and tools.

- Identify, develop and use reusable assets. This was primarily focused on a single specific project – the development of a product line; however, other projects were free to make use of any reusable assets that became available.

- Review procedures and evaluate results of experimental reuse project.

- Plan introduction of reuse-based improvements into regular practice.

- Preparation for reuse: (a) identify factors necessary to support introduction of planned reuse; (b) create technical environment to support reuse; (c) adapt working methods and foster corporate culture to support reuse; (d) formulate appropriate metrics for quantifying process improvements, and state specific improvement targets in terms of those metrics.

- Implementation of reuse: (a) construct initial library of reusable code to form the basis of applications development; (b) demonstrate use of reusable code in useful working applications; (c) demonstrate reuse applied to deliverables other than code. [Note. Implementation was piloted on two sub-projects which were part of developing the new product line. In the first, reuse was introduced after the analysis, design and initial coding had been completed; in the second, reuse was introduced right from the analysis stage.]

- Assessment of reuse: (a) using appropriate metrics, assess the likely longer-term impact of reuse on productivity, quality and maintenance; (b) evaluate the effectiveness of the steps taken to support reuse.

Eliop   ## Chase

Software Process Maturity

Independently of the reuse project, but concurrently with it, ELIOP obtained ISO-9001 certification for all its processes. At that time, the company had not undertaken any process maturity appraisals.

Chase has deliberately not undertaken any process maturity appraisals, not because of any opposition in principle, but from a pragmatic view that the effort outweighs the benefit. The driver for process improvement is business goals rather than compliance with an assessment model. The company informally rates itself as being at CMM maturity level 1. It is aware that not having a repeatable process makes it hard to measure benefits gained, and thus to justify changes in working practices, and remedying that is a longer-term process improvement goal.

Management

Good management of reuse, at both the business level and the software level, was treated as critically important. This was based on the recognition that (a) costs can escalate if not continuously controlled, and benefits may not be achieved unless they are kept always in view, (b) investment in reuse only yields benefits in the mid and long term, (c) there is thus a need for a business and product strategy looking beyond current projects, to anticipate needs and define product lines that will facilitate reuse. To reduce risks, an evolutionary step-by-step approach was preferred to revolutionary change.

It was recognized that any introduction of reuse requires senior management commitment in order to bring about the changes in outlook and working practice required. Management buy-in to reuse occurred before the start of the project, and all members of the management team were involved in the decision to embark on it. The reuse project had a high profile in the company, and was managed by a senior executive.

176

Eliop	Chase

Reuse Coordination and Tracking

Measurement was seen as essential in order to get feedback on the effects of change and to control it.

Key metrics were:

- extra cost of reusable assets, based on detailed project-oriented effort accounting;

- number of uses of reusable assets;

- software problems accounting, with problems weighted according to how critical they are and the phase when they appear.

Progress on the reuse project was reviewed by the senior executive responsible, and subsequently presented to the Executive Committee, leading to frank and open discussion of the project in management meetings.

Reuse Organization

Development is organized in teams, with one or more teams for each different software environment.

The introduction of reuse was organized as a project, with the following elements.

- Project manager, with overall responsibility for the reuse project.

- Reuse task group, made up of the project manager, two team heads and two senior engineers, responsible for high-level technical work, and for control and supervision of the reuse project.

- Individual software engineers, who undertook specific reuse

The company has a flat organizational structure, as appropriate to a small enterprise. All senior managers have multiple roles. Before the reuse project, development was organized into separate teams for each client. That changed during the project, with separate teams created for each phase of the process, each team working across all clients. Requirements analysts, or code developers, for example, now work with all clients, and thus know the reusable assets appropriate to their work. Continuity between phases is provided by a manager responsible for each client. Organizing the introduction of reuse as a separately staffed 'insulated' project was not practicable: staff were assigned

Eliop

Chase

Reuse Organization (continued)

tasks such as tool evaluation and installation.

specific reuse tasks from time to time, in parallel with their mainstream work on development projects.

Reuse Roles

ELIOP's decisions on roles during the reuse introduction project were the same as those made by Chase (see the right-hand column).

It was recognized that, as reuse is rolled out after the project, there would be a need for a specialist library administrator, and that project and team heads might need to be assigned specific responsibilities in promoting reuse.

During the reuse introduction project, the changes to existing roles were minimal. No reuse-specific activities were allocated on a full-time basis, either within the reuse project or among the mainstream developers. The project was managed on a part-time basis, and the project manager was in effect the reuse champion. An advantage of this approach was that it achieved maximum awareness and involvement throughout the development teams.

Human Aspects

Three key human issues were identified: total involvement by software developers – they must see benefits from reuse; understanding reusable assets – only an asset whose function, interface and restrictions are well understood can be successfully reused; and training.

Training activities were in three stages.

- Start of project: provide a wider vision of the different environments to developers that normally

Staff mainly fall into three categories.

- Senior managers with 30 years' experience in the computer industry, with little practical knowledge of current development methods, but with a strong commitment to improving the development process.

- Experienced developers, with a varying grasp of object orientation and reuse, but with a good knowledge of the existing development toolset.

Eliop

Chase

Human Aspects (continued)

work only in one specific environment. The aim was to facilitate horizontal reuse across environments. Later, the emphasis was switched to vertical reuse, and the initial horizontally-oriented training was then evaluated as not very relevant; it was nevertheless well accepted at the time it was given.

- Mid-project: provide essential knowledge of reuse concepts, the objectives and early findings of the project, and the methods and tools to be used (including practical use of the library system).

- End of project: gain acceptance for further planned process improvements, explain newly introduced metrics, discuss project conclusions. To achieve these aims, it was important to encourage active participation and open discussion.

- Recent graduates with a theoretical knowledge of object orientation and reuse, but little practical experience of commercial development. These are typically willing to learn, but tended to be reticent about contributing new ideas to the project.

Company culture was already changing from the entrepreneurial approach required for start-up to a more managed approach. The staff profile was changing from one of heroic hackers to a professional one. This more managed and professional approach led Chase to review its development process. Resistance to change was expected, first from those who did not see the benefits of reuse and wanted to keep working as they had been, and second from those responsible for delivering systems to clients on time. To combat resistance, (a) results and recommendations were disseminated through internal seminars and the introduction of new procedures into all projects, (b) each change was used in a small trial before being universally adopted, so that changes could be seen to benefit those involved (they often led to reductions in rework and, since rework is not popular, resistance was minimal). Where there was resistance it frequently resulted from the

Eliop	Chase

Human Aspects (continued)

feeling that changes were not radical enough!

Training was of two types: (a) in-house workshops, to disseminate knowledge gained on external courses, and to develop and promulgate ideas for process improvement from all staff; (b) external training on object-oriented development, and on using the inheritance properties of PowerBuilder.

The principal skills that have been acquired have been in identifying reuse possibilities. These skills were partially evolved in-house and partially through external courses. Once they were gathered, they were promulgated through internal workshops and reviews.

Processes

The following steps were taken.

- The whole process, including reuse, was documented.

- Requirements, design and testing documentation was revised.

- Templates and guidelines were produced for all major documents, and coding style rules were revised.

- Domain analysis was introduced into the process.

Prior to the reuse project, the development process for each new customer was to take an existing system, clone it and then adapt it. This approach meant that traceability between different customers' requirements was lost, making it hard to capitalize on the similarity between applications. Maintaining this growing number of different, though similar, systems threatened to become difficult.

In the revised process, each project generates defined deliverables,

Eliop

Chase

Processes (continued)

- Reviews of all assets were introduced.

compliant with defined standards, at key milestone points. As far as possible deliverables are generated from a catalogue of existing assets. They are not maintained by being directly edited, but indirectly through maintenance of the base assets.

Methods, Techniques and Technologies

It was recognized that reusability depends on high-quality assets, and that tools are an important determinant of quality, provided their contribution is well understood and planned. A range of tools were evaluated and selected, falling into two classes.

- Reuse-specific tools: a reusable software library. It was not possible to integrate the selected tool with the configuration management tool. Such integration is desirable because direct storage of components in the library causes problems when assets are changed; no suitable commercial tool was found featuring this integration, however. The software library was the biggest cause of resistance to the introduction of reuse, because it was slow and user-unfriendly.

- Non-reuse-specific tools: support for testing, portability, metrics and other general issues. Also, a

The core development tools (Analysts Workbench, PowerBuilder, Oracle, Business Objects) were in place before the project, and have remained in place. Previously a separate requirements model was created for each client; now there is a central requirements catalogue, and any new client-specific requirements are added to the catalogue. In code development, reuse is achieved through a combination of direct reuse, inheritance and parameterisation. Objects may be at a relatively low level, such as a drop-down field on a screen for selection from a table, or at a high level, such as inheriting a standard screen and just coding the differences.

The main changes to the technical environment are in quality assurance. When reusing assets it is essential that they conform to agreed standards, and the Cyrano tool has been introduced to monitor and report conformance to GUI and

Eliop

Chase

Methods, Techniques and Technologies (continued)

networked environment was necessary to share the needed information. Object oriented techniques were evaluated, leading to the conclusion that they have some advantages but are not essential.

development standards. Future changes are anticipated to the testing phase.

Assets

Types of reusable assets are: source and object code, specifications and design documents, testing procedures and testing reports. Source and object code can be held at module or subsystem level. The identification of reusable assets was done in two ways: assets for 'planned reuse' were identified as a result of domain analysis; assets for 'unplanned reuse' were identified from existing software.

Types of reusable assets are: requirements catalogue, master process model, detailed process descriptions, data model, window formats, menus, and code objects. It is intended to add test plans, procedures, cases and scripts.

- Assets for planned reuse. Domain analysis was identified as the key activity for planned reuse. A domain analysis experiment was defined on a specific product line, and conducted by a senior software engineer with good knowledge of the domain. People in the marketing and commercial areas were identified as additional sources of knowledge. The domain model had a structure very similar to the specifications and high-level design documents already in use. This had two advantages: it fitted the existing culture, and

Eliop

Chase

Assets (continued)

specifications and designs for actual products were easy to derive. The domain analysis yielded 27 reusable generic source code assets (total 22 KLOC), and ten reusable documents (total 318 pages).

- Assets for unplanned reuse. Selecting existing assets to be reusable was considered necessary in order to create a sufficient critical mass to encourage developers to search for reusable assets with a reasonable probability of success. The following activities were undertaken. (a) Evaluate assets for reusability (criteria were: general quality, including compliance to in-house standards; usefulness; maintainability; maturity; genericity. (b) Adapt assets for reuse. (c) Add to library. Because the quality criteria exceeded the average quality level of existing assets, only a relatively small number were selected: 74 source code modules (total 49 KLOC) and 48 documents (total 864 pages).

Repository

After searching unsuccessfully for a valid commercial tool, a library system was implemented using standard database management software, to hold reference information about assets. Most assets are

Since the requirements catalogue is used by a small team, who can all be aware of all components, it is maintained manually. The approach to detailed analysis and design documents is similar. Code objects are

Eliop	**Chase**

Repository (continued)

stored in a separate repository using a configuration management tool; those not under configuration management are stored in the library. The library generates usage metrics (number of retrievals and modifications). Each asset has an identification, reference data, description, keywords, projects in which asset used, related assets, and size metrics. Where source code has real-time or concurrence constraints, making it only reusable under the same operating system and similar hardware, information is held on the constraints and the operating platform. A user-friendly interface for the library was identified as a major need, and the first version of the tool needed enhancement to its user interface in order to improve user acceptance.

managed through configuration management software and a tool-based library of descriptions.

Actual Reuse Results

The main conclusions from the experimental reuse project were: (a) reuse should become part of regular software development practice; (b) software process improvement should be established as a continuing activity, with yearly objectives and budgets.

Benefits in the form of cost savings are hard to estimate even when good historical cost data is available, because one has to compare the real

Reuse is now central to the development approach. It is incorporated in all phases of the process, with review points ensuring that reuse possibilities are always considered. The process is improved in terms of time to market, reduced demand on scarce resources (particularly through reductions in rework), product quality, and client confidence.

Due to the poor process repeatability at the start of the reuse project,

Eliop

Chase

Actual Reuse Results (continued)

situation with reuse against a hypothetical situation without reuse. A 10–20 per cent improvement can be masked by other factors (variations in skills and experience, errors in estimating project size and complexity, customer influence etc.). Rough estimates were nevertheless attempted. The following figures relate to planned reuse, and are compared to a notional standard cost of 100.

	1st use	2nd use	3rd use	4th use
Accumulated cost	160	180	190	200
Cost per use	160	90	63	50

Thus, savings may appear on second use. The results should be interpreted carefully, however, for several reasons. (a) It is assumed that the alternative to planned reuse is no reuse; if the alternative is unplanned reuse, the relative benefits will decrease. (b) No provision is made for lower maintenance cost. (c) Part of the initial extra cost is due to the immaturity of the newly introduced practices, including a tendency to make reusable asset specifications unnecessarily complex. For unplanned reuse, the average effort needed to select and adapt assets was measured at 5 hours per KLOC for code and 0.2 hours per page for documents – a small fraction of the effort needed to produce the asset initially; and these efforts will

comparative metrics are difficult to produce. Initial, qualitative and subjective estimates suggest that the extra cost to implement reuse is around 20 per cent if undertaken during initial development, and around 75 per cent if undertaken as subsequent retrofitting. Savings where reusable assets are used in later projects may be as much as 50 per cent, depending on the degree of commonality.

The largest cultural change has been the acceptance of process improvement as a way of life. Software processes are better understood and subject to frequent scrutiny. Although the main aim of the project was to introduce reuse, perhaps this acceptance of process improvement will be the most important long-term benefit.

The benefits have been realized and recognized to the extent that plans were already in place at the end of the project to extend reuse (especially within the testing phase) and to continue process improvement. As part of the continuing drive to improve, Chase is considering the investigation of process maturity measures to track where improvements should be targeted. It is unlikely that a full CMM model will be used, but a pragmatic subset may be identified in order to monitor and track future improvements.

Eliop	Chase

Actual Reuse Results (continued)

decrease as better quality procedures are introduced. The estimates do not provide, however, for the effort of modifying assets for reuse, or for the probability that the asset will actually be reused (a low probability of reuse will increase costs). The major conclusion on costs is that large savings are unlikely, and that quality is a far more important benefit.

It was clear (a) that reuse promotes better quality, (b) that quality is a prerequisite for reuse: a positive feedback loop thus exists between quality and reuse. Only good quality software from a good quality process can be successfully reused. Barriers to reuse are closely related to poor quality and bad practices. If they are removed, reuse becomes feasible and generates quality gains. Reuse is thus recommended as part of a quality improvement program.

Conclusion

The two companies operate in very different application domains – industrial control and marine insurance; but they have software groups that are very similar in size. Drivers and expectations, and the approaches to introducing reuse, were also similar.

Neither company has undertaken process maturity assessments, or has a process improvement programme in place.

In each company a senior manager acted as an effective champion of reuse, and there was strong commitment and involvement by the rest of management. Both companies organized the introduction of reuse as a project, but with participation on a part-time basis from staff primarily occupied on 'front-line' development, thus achieving total involvement.

Templates and standards have been introduced by both companies. Eliop has introduced domain analysis into its process, whereas Chase starts from a standard domain model: this probably reflects a different degree of variability in their respective customer requirements, but both companies are aiming at high leverage by starting at the requirements and architecture stage, and they both identify a wide range of reusable asset types.

Eliop distinguishes between the planned reuse of newly-developed assets and the unplanned reuse of pre-existing asset stock; that distinction is not made by Chase, probably because the introduction of reuse was closely contemporary with the development of a new product line in which earlier assets would have had limited value. The two companies' technical environments are quite different. Chase links reuse with object orientation, whereas Eliop does not, and they have a contrasting use of supporting tools. Eliop takes a more formal approach to the cataloguing and storing of assets by use of a repository.

Both companies have experienced difficulties with showing measurable results of reuse, but both are certain of its benefits. They are both committed to the long-term continuation and extension of reuse, and to embedding it in a wider programme of software process improvement.

Experience Review and Success Factors

10

ABSTRACT

The reuse experience base created for this book contains data on projects undertaken in nineteen companies which have embarked on significant reuse programmes. This concluding Chapter provides a synthesis of that collected experience, in terms of recurring patterns and success/failure factors.

(Note: this Chapter is an adapted and abbreviated version of a paper that has been published in *IEEE Transactions on Software Engineering.*)

10.1 The Experience Base

The survey on which the experience reports in this book are based covered 24 projects, all of which were undertaking reuse seriously for the first time. The projects were carried out in 19 European companies.

For each company, the source of data was a report and an interview. Interviews were performed by one or two interviewers in each case, and lasted between two and three hours. They were based on a standard questionnaire, a copy of which was given to interviewees in advance. Interviewees were guaranteed confidentiality of the data provided, unless they granted specific permission for it to be associated with their companies.

Interview reports were sent to interviewees for their approval. Finally, the reports were coded on the basis of a number of variables. Some of the variables had predetermined codes, so that coding was in fact performed directly during the interviews. In other cases the variables and codes were reorganized and changed after the interviews (post-formed codes). Codes were assigned on the basis of discussion and agreement between members of the survey team. The resulting data sets are shown in Tables 10.1, 10.2 and 10.3. Confidentiality is maintained by using alphabetic project identifiers.

Each data point (a row in the tables) corresponds to one project. In each table, the darker shaded rows depict projects that were judged to have failed, while unshaded rows correspond to successful projects. The definition of failure and success will be discussed later.

Each data point has a number of variables. They are divided between *state variables* (attributes over which a company has no control, such as size and application domain, presented in Table 10.1) and *control variables* (attributes a company can control, such as commitment of management, modifications to the process, reuse approach etc., presented in Tables 10.2 and 10.3).

Table 10.1, showing the values of the state variables for each of the 24 projects, follows. The meanings and values of the state variables (column headings) are now defined.

software staff (number of staff involved in software development)
S	small (1–50)
M	medium (51–200)
L	large (>201)

overall staff (number of staff in the company)
S	small (1–50)
M	medium (51–200)
L	large (201–500)
X	extra-large (>501)

type of software production
isolated	the company develops projects that have little or nothing in common
product family	the company develops a set of software products that are tailored to the requirements of different customers and/or evolve over time

software and product (software/end-product relationship)
alone	the software constitutes a standalone product
process	the software is embedded in a process
product	the software is embedded in a product

software process maturity (actual or estimated)
high	CMM level 3 or higher
middle	ISO 9001 certification or CMM level 2
low	no ISO 9001 certification or CMM level 1

190

Table 10.1 The experience base: state variables.

Project identifier	Software staff	Over-all staff	Type of software production	Software and product	Software process maturity	Application domain	Type of software	Size of base-line	Development approach	Staff experience
A	L	L	product family	product	high	telecommunications	technical	L	OO	high
B	L	L	product family	product	high	telecommunications	technical	M	OO	high
D	L	L	isolated	alone	middle	software tools	technical	M	OO	middle
E	L	L	isolated	alone	middle	telecommunications	technical	M	OO	middle
F	L	L	isolated	alone	middle	telecommunications	technical	M	OO	middle
G	L	X	product family	process	low	banking	business	L	OO	middle
H	M	M	product family	product	high	engine control	embedded RT	L	OO	middle
I	M	X	product family	product	middle	flight mgmt systems	technical	M	OO	high
J	M	X	product family	product	middle	flight mgmt systems	technical	M	OO	middle
K	M	X	product family	product	middle	air traffic control	non-embedded RT	L	proc	high
L	M	X	product family	product	high	train simulation	technical	M	proc	high
M	M	X	product family	product	high	software tools	technical	L	proc	middle
N	M	X	product family	product	middle	train traffic control	non-embedded RT	M	proc	middle
O	S	L	product family	product	middle	space	embedded RT	M	OO	middle
P	S	M	product family	product	middle	manufacturing	embedded RT	M	proc	middle
Q	S	M	product family	product	middle	manufacturing	technical	M	proc	middle
R	S	M	product family	product	middle	telecommunications	embedded RT	L	proc	high
S	S	S	product family	product	low	measurement	technical	M	OO	middle
T	S	X	product family	product	middle	flight mgmt systems	embedded RT	M	OO	high
U	S	X	product family	process	low	finance	business	L	OO	low
V	S	X	product family	product	low	telecommunications	technical	S	OO	middle
W	M	L	product family	alone	middle	manufacturing	business	L	OO	middle
X	S	S	product family	NA	low	book-keeping	business	S	proc	middle
Y	M	M	isolated	product	high	flight mgmt systems	embedded RT	not available	not available	not available

application domain
  measurement management and control of measurement environment
           (other values self-explanatory)

type of software
  embedded RT embedded real-time
  non-
  embedded RT non-embedded real-time
  technical   non-embedded non-real-time, limited DBMS, significant
           control part
  business   non-embedded non-real-time, significant DBMS, limited
           control part

size of baseline (size of the host project on which reuse was applied)
  S   small (<10 KLOC and/or 10 person-months effort)
  M   medium (10–100 KLOC and/or 10–100 person-months)
  L   large (100–500 KLOC and/or more than 100 person-
          months)

development approach (analysis and design approach used in the project)
  OO   object-oriented
  proc   procedural

staff experience (average development experience of software staff)
  high   5 years or more
  middle 2–4 years
  low   1 year or less

Note: NA (project X) stands for 'not applicable'. The same abbreviation is also used in Tables 10.2 and 10.3.

Small and medium companies are fairly represented in the experience base, the smallest being a ten-person software house. As far as we know small companies have not previously reported their reuse experience in the literature. It is reasonable to suppose that this was due not to their absence from the arena, but to not having the resources to publish.

Under *software production, product family* outnumbers *isolated* by five to one. *Product family* (see definition above) does not necessarily mean that the company is using a domain engineering approach to technical development or a product line approach in their business. It simply means that the majority of the companies surveyed recognize the commonality in their products and have become interested in reuse as a consequence.

In *software and product,* only one-sixth of the cases deal with software that is not embedded in products or processes. That could be interpreted as reflecting an increasing spread of embedded software in products and processes as opposed to standalone products. Alternatively it could suggest that, compared to standalone software, software embedded in a range of products or processes provides more favourable conditions for reuse.

Taking the above two variables (*software production* and *software and product*) together, 20 out of the 24 cases are product family, and 17 are product-embedded. The straightforward conclusion is that organisations tend to identify product families where they produce product-embedded software, and that the combination of these two related characteristics seems to offer natural conditions for reuse.

As far as *software process maturity* is concerned, only five of the projects were developed in organisational units judged to be of low maturity.

Under *application domain*, the predominance of telecommunications (six cases) is noteworthy.

Under *type of software*, the prevalence (half the cases) is of technical applications, ie non-embedded non-real-time, with limited or no database and an important algorithmic or control part. Overall, 20 of the 24 projects could be described as being of a software engineering nature, with only 4 being of an information systems nature. The cause of this bias could be intrinsic to the nature of the software in the two domains, or intrinsic to the differing software development cultures, or a combination of the two.

In terms of *development approach, object-oriented* outweighs *procedural* by two to one.

As far as *staff experience* is concerned, only one of the projects was performed by a group of beginners with average development experience of less than one year. Companies generally assigned projects involving reuse to their more experienced staff.

In summary, most of the companies in the experience base produce software embedded in products or processes, with reasonable levels of commonality between applications and adequately mature processes, and they assign experienced staff to reuse projects. Both procedural and object-oriented development approaches are well represented. They thus satisfy some of the important assumed prerequisites for successful reuse. In practice, however, nearly 40 per cent of the projects (the shaded rows in Table 10.1) were judged to have resulted in failure.

To try to understand the reasons for success or failure, it is necessary to turn to the control variables – those characteristics that are under the influence of a company's own decision processes.

Control variables have been divided into two categories: high-level and low-level. High-level control variables correspond to decisions that (whether taken explicitly or by default) subsequently influence low-level control variables. They are shown in Table 10.2 and defined below. As before, the darker shaded rows represent projects that are judged to have failed.

top management commitment
   yes   top management of the company had a clear commitment to introducing and sustaining reuse
   no   top management did not show that commitment, so that reuse was initiated from middle managers and/or technical staff

key reuse roles introduced
   yes   at least one reuse role (such as reuse programme manager, asset owner, library manager, asset producer) was introduced
   no   no reuse roles were introduced

Table 10.2 The experience base: high-level control variables.

Project identifier	Top management commitment	Key reuse roles introduced	Reuse processes introduced	Non-reuse processes modified	Repository	Human factors
A	yes	yes	yes	yes	yes	yes
B	yes	yes	yes	yes	yes	yes
D	yes	yes	no	no	yes	no
E	yes	yes	no	no	yes	no
F	yes	yes	no	no	yes	no
G	yes	yes	yes	yes	yes	yes
H	yes	yes	yes	yes	yes	yes
I	no	no	no	yes	yes	no
J	no	no	no	yes	yes	no
K	yes	yes	yes	yes	yes	yes
L	yes	yes	yes	yes	yes	yes
M	yes	yes	yes	yes	yes	yes
N	yes	yes	yes	yes	yes	yes
O	yes	no	no	no	yes	no
P	yes	yes	yes	yes	yes	yes
Q	yes	yes	yes	yes	yes	yes
R	yes	yes	yes	yes	yes	yes
S	yes	yes	yes	yes	yes	yes
T	no	yes	yes	no	yes	no
U	yes	yes	no	yes	yes	yes
V	yes	yes	yes	yes	yes	yes
W	yes	no	yes	no	yes	yes
X	yes	NA	NA	NA	NA	no
Y	no	yes	no	no	yes	yes

reuse processes introduced

  yes   at least one reuse-specific process (such as domain analysis, qual-
          ification, classification) was introduced

  no   no reuse-specific processes were introduced

non-reuse processes modified

  yes   at least one non-reuse-specific process (such as requirements
          analysis, design, testing) was modified

  no   no non-reuse-specific processes were modified

repository

  yes   assets were stored in an asset repository, supported by a tool (not
          necessarily a dedicated reuse repository tool)

  no   no asset repository was established

human factors

  yes   human factors were considered and dealt with (for instance via
          awareness, training and motivation actions)

  no   human factors were not considered

Values of the high-level control variables represent the combination of key
high-level management decisions about a reuse programme. For instance, in
case A it was a top management decision to embark on reuse; a reuse group
was set up, both to produce reusable assets and to support reusers; the software development process was modified appropriately; a repository for
assets was set up; and training and awareness actions were undertaken to
support the transition.

In case T, in contrast, the reuse programme started as an initiative by middle-
level managers. A repository was set up, a library manager was appointed
and legacy work products were placed in the repository. However, no modifications were made to existing processes, and no actions were taken to
spread awareness of the reuse programme.

While a *no* on a high-level control variable means no action (whether by
explicit decision or by default), a *yes* may represent a whole range of possible
more detailed actions. The low-level control variables represent those more
detailed lower-level decisions on how to implement reuse initiatives that
appeared in the cases in the experience base. They are shown in Table 10.3
and are defined below.

reuse approach

  loose   reusable work products are independent, and are typically reused
            in isolation without a common defined architecture

  tight   reusable work products are designed to be closely related, so that
            reuse of one work product typically involves reusing a wider set

195

Table 10.3 The experience base: low-level control variables.

Project identifier	Reuse approach	Work products	Domain analysis	Origin	Independent team	When assets Developed	Qualification	Configuration management	Rewards policy	Number of assets
A	tight	D+C	yes	ex novo	yes	before	yes	yes	no	51–100
B	tight	D+C	yes	ex novo	yes	before	yes	yes	no	51–100
D	loose	C	no	as-is	no	before	no	no	yes	21–50
E	loose	C	no	as-is	no	before	no	no	yes	21–50
F	loose	C	no	as-is	no	before	no	no	yes	21–50
G	loose	C	no	reeng	no	just in time	yes	yes	no	51–100
H	tight	R+D+C	no	reeng	no	just in time	no	yes	no	51–100
I	loose	D+C	no	reeng	no	just in time	no	no	no	51–100
J	loose	D+C	no	reeng	no	just in time	no	no	no	51–100
K	tight	R+D+C	yes	reeng	no	just in time	yes	yes	no	100+
L	tight	R+D+C	yes	reeng	no	just in time	yes	yes	no	51–100
M	tight	R+D+C	yes	reeng	no	just in time	yes	yes	no	100+
N	tight	R+D+C	yes	reeng	no	just in time	yes	yes	no	51–100
O	loose	R+D+C	no	ex novo	no	before	yes	yes	no	1–20
P	loose	R+D+C	yes	reeng	no	just in time	yes	yes	no	100+
Q	loose	R+D+C	yes	reeng	no	just in time	yes	yes	no	100+
R	loose	C	no	reeng	no	just in time	yes	yes	no	1–20
S	tight	C	no	ex novo	no	just in time	yes	yes	no	100+
T	loose	C	no	reeng	no	just in time	yes	yes	no	1–20
U	tight	R+D+C	no	reeng	no	just in time	no	yes	no	100+
V	tight	C	no	reeng	no	just in time	yes	yes	no	1–20
W	tight	C	yes	reeng	no	just in time	no	no	no	1–20
X	NA	NA	NA	NA	NA	NA	NA	NA	no	NA
Y	loose	C	no	as-is	no	before	no	no	no	100+

work products (types of assets reused)
- C　　　code
- D　　　design
- R　　　requirements
- C+D　　code and design
　　　　　etc.

domain analysis
- *yes*　　domain analysis is performed
- *no*　　domain analysis is not performed

origin
- *as-is*　　reusable assets are existing work products, reused without modification

ex novo reusable assets are developed from scratch

reeng reusable assets are developed by reengineering existing work products

independent team

yes reusable assets are developed by a team that is independent from the development projects that may use them

no development project teams both develop reusable assets and use them

when assets developed

before reusable assets are developed well before a development project may use them

just in reusable assets are developed just before a development project

time will use them

qualification

yes assets undergo a defined qualification process to be certified as reusable

no assets do not undergo a defined qualification process to be certified as reusable

configuration management

yes reusable assets are under configuration management and change control

no reusable assets are not under configuration management and change control

rewards policy

yes a rewards policy to promote reuse is in place

no a rewards policy to promote reuse is not in place

number of assets (estimated number of reusable assets in the repository) (self-explanatory)

Different combinations of values for these low-level control variables represent specific approaches to the implementation of reuse. For instance, in case A a dedicated group produces object-oriented frameworks with documented designs. These assets are produced from scratch, some time before projects need them. Work products are subjected to a qualification process and are under configuration control.

Case R is also judged successful, but works quite differently. When a project developing an application identifies a legacy subprogram that could be reused by the same project and by others, it reengineers it for reusability and quality.

The tight approach to reuse (as defined under *reuse approach*) requires further elaboration. This approach is normally associated with object-oriented and framework technology, but some companies used it with traditional procedural technology. It consists in engineering a generic product that mirrors the specific business of the company. The generic product is then instantiated and customized for each different customer or application. Reusing a generic product means that a standard architecture is defined and its use enforced. The tight approach does not exclude use of the loose approach when suitable. We found several different forms of tight approach.

- Domain analysis with frameworks (projects A, B, W). After a domain analysis effort, one or more frameworks are built (A, B) or reengineered from legacy (W) and maintained. The reusable asset unit is the framework, with its related documentation. Object-oriented technology is used extensively.

- Product baseline (projects H, K, L, M, N, U). The generic product is built with procedural technology, and maintained over time as a sequence of versions in a configuration management system. Specific instances for customers are derived from the product baseline, by additions, deletions and modifications. The product baseline is built using domain analysis (K, L, M, N) or less formally using the know-how of senior designers (H, U). The reusable asset is the product baseline, with its related documentation.

- Composition language (project S). One company has defined source-code work products and a language for assembling them. The reusable asset is the subset of work products selected by the directives of the composition language.

Finally, a word on success and failure. Success is judged according to a combination of three chief criteria: the continuation of the reuse programme after the completion of the baseline project in which it was introduced, the degree to which assets were actually reused, and the subjective assessment of those involved in the projects. It would be desirable to use some more quantitative measure such as return on investment; only one company attempted such a measure, however, and even when such measures are used it is difficult to know how comparable they are between one company and another. It is notable that, in almost every one of the projects shown to have been failures, the failure was openly admitted and discussed by the interviewees.

10.2 Analysis of Experience

This Section reports the results of three different analyses of the data assembled in Tables 10.1, 10.2 and 10.3 above. The three analyses are presented below under the headings 'Successes and failures in general', 'Successes in more detail' and 'Failures in more detail'. The essential nature of each analysis, and the difference between them, is as follows.

'Successes and failures in general' covers all 24 cases and investigates the effect of the state variables (Table 10.1) and the high-level control variables (Table 10.2) on success or failure. The analysis shows that not addressing two or more high-level control variables led to failure. Of the state variables, only *Type of software production* has an impact.

'Successes in more detail' covers only the fifteen successful cases, and investigates the relationship between the state variables (Table 10.1) and the low-level control variables (Table 10.3). As we know from qualitative data from interviews, successful projects solved the reuse equation in a variety of ways. This is captured by the variety of values taken by the low-level control variables. Is there a regularity in the diversity of approaches to reuse? Do state variables influence the approach?

'Failures in more detail' covers the nine unsuccessful cases. As noted, failure was normally clear to interviewees, who openly discussed the causes. These discussions typically went beyond the points in the questionnaire, and in most cases identified the root causes of failure. Root cause analyses for each failure are presented, and two common failure scenarios are derived.

10.2.1 Successes and Failures in General

This analysis covers all twenty-four cases and investigates the effect of the state variables (Table 10.1) and the high-level control variables (Table 10.2) on success or failure. In both figures failures are indicated by shaded rows.

An examination of the high-level control variables in Table 10.2 shows that successful projects typically have *yes* values, the only exceptions being projects U and W. Projects that failed have three or more *no* values.

Combining the result of that visual analysis of the data set with further insights from the interviews leads to the following tentative conclusions.

● All high-level control variables are important for a successful reuse programme.

- Introducing reuse processes and modifying non-reuse processes are key points for successfully producing and consuming assets.

- Top management commitment is a prerequisite for successfully achieving process change.

- Human factors must be addressed to sustain process change from the bottom up.

- Introducing key reuse roles, and setting up a repository, are neither in themselves sufficient for successful reuse. That is not to say that they are unimportant. The key point is that both represent relatively minor changes in a company, which can be accomplished with partial management support. As a result they are done in most projects, but cannot, by themselves alone, induce the major changes needed.

Of the state variables, only *type of software production* has an effect. Most of the cases with value *product family*, in contrast with none of the cases with value *isolated*, were successful. Since there are only four *isolated* cases in the sample, it is not possible to conclude that such cases are never suitable for reuse, especially since none of them took enough account of the issues addressed by the high-level control variables. The probability is that *isolated* cases could achieve success, provided they are specially careful to take account of the high-level control variables.

Size, in terms of both *software staff* and *overall staff*, does not appear to be a conditioning factor. However, size impacts indirectly on two things.

- First is the ease or difficulty for achieving top management commitment, and its propagation to lower hierarchical levels. Successful smaller companies (projects P, Q, R, S) have the advantage of easier communication of information (for instance information about reusable assets, domains and projects is more easily shared among the staff) and easier building of consensus for the reuse programme (the programme is initiated when the occupier of a prominent role in the company – owner, director, technical lead – decides accordingly). Failure in two projects (O, T) happened in two small software organisations belonging to large non-software companies. In those cases commitment from management of the small software organisation was not sufficient to remove obstacles at the upper level.

- The other is the reuse organization. Successful smaller companies (projects P, Q, R, S) find leaner organisations are adequate to support reuse processes (generation of assets, qualification, maintenance, domain analysis). Roles dedicated to reuse have necessarily to be part-time. The

200

production of assets is made on demand. Failure in a small company (project X) was due to defining a reuse infrastructure that was too complex, with complex procedures and full-time roles.

Other state variables that do not appear to be predictive of success or failure nevertheless merit some discussion.

Successful cases show a spread of *software process maturity* values from *high* to *low*. It may be assumed that process maturity is a useful but not necessary or sufficient factor in achieving success.

Type of software = embedded RT shows three cases of success and two of failure. Interview evidence suggests that the key distinguishing factor among the five cases is the presence in the failure cases of problems arising from hardware changes and performance constraints.

Development approach = OO shows an equal division between success and failure. The common notion that object orientation on its own is enough to guarantee successful reuse is thus shown to be false.

10.2.2 Successes in More Detail

This analysis covers only the fifteen successful cases, and investigates the relationship between the state variables (Table 10.1) and the low-level control variables (Table 10.3).

All the successful reuse initiatives addressed a common set of issues, as captured by the high-level control variables, and that was a key element of their success. But the precise way of addressing that set of issues, as captured by the low-level control variables, was fairly diverse.

The first question is whether some recurring pattern can be recognized among low-level control variables. If yes, are such patterns related to any of the state variables? For instance, do small companies tend to use pattern X, while large companies use pattern Y?

To explore this a subset of the experience base was created, limited to successful projects, a selection of the state variables, and the low-level control variables. Of the state variables, *type of software production* and *rewards policy* were omitted because all successful projects have the same values for them, and *application type* and *size of baseline* were omitted because the values for them seemed to be randomly related to success or failure.

Table 10.4 shows the reduced data set. The thick vertical line divides state variables (on the left) and low-level control variables (on the right).

Table 10.4 Success cases: state and low-level control variables.

Project identifier	Software staff	Over-all staff	Software and product	Software process maturity	Type of software	Development approach	Staff experience	Reuse approach	Work products	Domain analysis	Origin	Independent team	When asset developed	Qualification	Configuration management	Number of assets
A	L	L	product	high	technical	OO	high	tight	D+C	yes	ex novo	yes	before	yes	yes	51–100
B	L	L	product	high	technical	OO	high	tight	D+C	yes	ex novo	yes	before	yes	yes	51–100
G	L	X	process	low	business	OO	middle	loose	C	no	reeng	no	just in time	yes	yes	51–100
H	M	M	product	high	embedded RT	OO	middle	tight	R+D+C	no	reeng	no	just in time	no	yes	51–100
K	M	X	product	middle	non-embedded RT	proc	high	tight	R+D+C	yes	reeng	no	just in time	yes	yes	100+
L	M	X	product	high	technical	proc	high	tight	R+D+C	yes	reeng	no	just in time	yes	yes	51–100
M	M	X	product	high	technical	proc	middle	tight	R+D+C	yes	reeng	no	just in time	yes	yes	100+
N	M	X	product	middle	non-embedded RT	proc	middle	tight	R+D+C	yes	reeng	no	just in time	yes	yes	100+
P	S	M	product	middle	embedded RT	proc	middle	tight	R+D+C	yes	reeng	no	just in time	yes	yes	100+
Q	S	M	product	middle	embedded RT	proc	middle	loose	R+D+C	yes	reeng	no	just in time	yes	yes	100+
R	S	M	product	middle	technical	proc	high	loose	C	no	reeng	no	just in time	yes	yes	1–20
S	S	S	product	low	embedded RT	OO	middle	loose	C	no	ex novo	no	just in time	yes	yes	100+
U	S	X	process	low	technical	OO	low	tight	R+D+C	no	reeng	no	just in time	no	yes	100+
V	S	X	product	low	business	OO	middle	tight	C	no	reeng	no	just in time	yes	yes	1–20
W	M	L	alone	middle	business	OO	middle	tight	C	yes	reeng	no	just in time	no	no	1–20

Visual analysis of the data set is now more complex. It is readily possible to recognize a cluster comprising cases A and B, and another group comprising the rest, differentiated by the values for the variables *origin, when asset developed* and *independent team*: A and B are the only cases featuring an independent group for developing reusable assets, starting from scratch, with a tight approach. These two cases, both from the same company, represent an approach to reuse (which could be labelled 'sophisticated') requiring substantial levels of reorganization and investment. The other cases (which could be labelled 'pragmatic') have no independent team; they develop assets just in time, in most cases by reengineering. From the data available it is not possible to evaluate which approach produced better results. One can argue that this may not be important, since each approach was adapted to its organisational context and produced positive results.

Digging more into the 'pragmatic' cases, G and R share a loose approach, limit themselves to reuse of code and do not use domain analysis. However, there is a lot of variation in the values of those three variables across the other cases, and it is hard to identify meaningful patterns.

Overall, merging this analysis with insight from the interviews, it is possible to propose a main distinction between the 'sophisticated' and 'pragmatic' approaches, combined with the observation that a variety of approaches are possible under the 'pragmatic' umbrella. The important thing is that approaches should be adapted to the organisational context.

As far as state variables are concerned, it is hard to find meaningful patterns of correspondence between values of the state variables and the adoption of the sophisticated or pragmatic approach. The variables in the data set do not capture information that might be necessary to establish such correspondences, and the data set is anyway too small for correspondences to have a chance of becoming apparent.

It is possible to say tentatively that cases A and B chose the sophisticated approach because management decided to invest deeply in reuse, as one of the key technologies for the success of the company; the large size of the company meant that more resources were available and the sophisticated approach became feasible. The pragmatic approach in the other cases represented perhaps a degree of prudence, in which size was a factor: smaller companies face real constraints in allocating resources, which forces them in the direction of leaner organisations, with part-time reuse roles, and production of assets on demand.

10.2.3 Failures in More Detail

This analysis covers the nine unsuccessful cases. They are divided into four groups: DEF, IJY, OT and X.

In the case of project X, the reuse initiative was interrupted before completion because the company recognized it could not achieve its objectives. On the one hand, the objectives were too ambitious, especially given the small size of the company. On the other hand, factors extraneous to the reuse initiative intervened, such as key personnel turnover and crises in project management. The project is listed in the data set for completeness, but it is not used in the following analysis, since several fields are incomplete because of its premature termination.

Projects D, E and F accompanied the introduction of reuse with two major changes. First, they introduced a company-wide intranet-based repository, along with creating the role of repository manager responsible for documentation and version control of assets. Second, they introduced a complex policy for rewarding the producers and consumers of assets, in an attempt to create an internal market of assets. On the other hand, no changes were made to existing processes, either for the consumers or for the producers of assets. The assumption was also made that object orientation in itself would lead to effective reuse. It turned out that few assets were produced (mostly for small functions) and few, if any, were reused. The lesson from these projects is that installing a repository and a rewards policy alone are not enough to achieve systematic reuse.

In these three projects, the root causes of failure were the misconceptions that reuse is to be equated with establishing a repository and adopting an object-oriented approach. The secondary causes were the failure to modify non-reuse-specific processes and introduce reuse-specific ones, and the absence of any training and awareness actions.

Turning to projects I, J and Y: in case Y, the company set up an automated repository and filled it with legacy assets from past projects (mostly small-grained functions not specific to a single domain). In cases I and J a loosely formalized repository was set up to contain a limited number of purpose-built assets. In all three cases, no modification of non-reuse processes took place, no systematic production of assets was initiated, and no assets were ever reused. Not modifying non-reuse processes, and insufficiently publicizing the repository and the reuse initiative, were the immediate causes of failure. The root cause was probably the weak involvement of top management in the reuse initiative, leading to an absence of will and power to change existing processes.

In these three projects, very similarly to the previous three, the root causes of failure were an absence of top management commitment, and the misconception that reuse is to be equated with establishing a repository. The secondary causes were the failure to modify non-reuse-specific processes, the failure to produce reusable assets, and the absence of any training and awareness actions.

Projects O and T both produced embedded real-time software and were both subcontracts in bigger projects. Each tried to address the introduction of reuse-specific processes and the modification of non-reuse-specific processes. However, they were not able to achieve those changes, since they were subcontractors and they did not own all the processes. Moreover, because of performance constraints imposed on the embedded real-time software, they could not use the well-known technique of de-coupling software from hardware using layers. As a result, reusable assets were produced, but could never be reused because of changes to requirements, both in functionality and hardware. In the end the reuse initiatives were abandoned. Both projects agreed reuse could have been achieved in their context, but only if started at the level of the main contractor. The lesson here is that a subcontractor can rarely decide to go for reuse independently of the main contractor, especially in the delicate case of embedded real-time software. Embedded real-time software is not a cause of failure *per se*, however, as demonstrated by other successful cases (projects H, P and R).

In these two cases, the root causes of failure were the effects of memory and speed constraints in the embedded real-time systems that were being developed, and the customer-contractor relationship. The secondary cause was that, while reusable assets were produced, they were never used.

Among the failures analysed above, two similar sets of projects can be recognized. Projects D, E, F, I, J and Y failed primarily because of misconceptions. Projects O and T failed primarily because of the context – embedded real-time software and a customer-contractor environment. Two failure scenarios can thus be hypothesised corresponding to those two sets. They are by no means the only possible scenarios: more could be identified by observing other projects.

● Failure scenario 1 (cases D, E, F, I, J and Y)

All these failures are in some way related to the misconception that installing a repository is the key point in a reuse programme, and/or that object-orientation automatically leads to successful reuse. In some cases (I and J) management did not fully support the reuse initiative. Those points are related: setting up a repository is a relatively easy and non-intrusive task that can be performed off-line, without interfering deeply with everyday processes. More serious changes require top management commitment. However, top management commitment exists in half the failure cases and is absent in the other half, so it is not possible to conclude that its absence alone inevitably leads to failure.

Root cause of failure	Misconceptions (reuse = repository, reuse = OO)
Secondary causes of failure	No non-reuse-specific processes modified No reuse-specific processes installed No training/awareness

- Failure scenario 2 (cases O and T)

No further discussion is needed beyond that already provided.

Root causes of failure	Embedded RT system context (memory and speed constraints) Customer – contractor context (no ownership of choices on hardware and requirements)
Secondary cause of failure	No reusable assets available

10.3 A Reuse Introduction Decision Sequence

The results of the previous analysis can now be exploited by presenting a decision sequence. The decision sequence tries to learn from the cases in the experience base and does not claim scientific validity as a prediction tool for new cases. However, it highlights issues that should be considered when starting a reuse programme.

1. *Reuse potential*

    Evaluate the reuse potential, which is much higher when similar software products are produced over time (*type of software production = product family*). In practice this is not an easy task, as it involves identifying the functions likely to be reused, and the number of times they could be reused within a given time period. Several techniques, under the heading of domain analysis and product lines (Bayer *et al.*, 1999[1]; Weiss and Lai, 1999[2]), have been proposed to guide this task.

2. *Reuse capability*

Get the commitment of top management to obtain resources and power to change non-reuse-specific processes, add reuse-specific processes, address human factors, and set up a repository. Those points are not in a significant order: they should all be addressed. When two or more of them are not addressed, a failure is likely. Adding reuse-specific processes normally implies defining and assigning key reuse roles, and so that is an additional implicit requirement. The factor common to all of them is *change*, which is why the prerequisite is commitment from top management. Another prerequisite is knowing what the processes are. Here two factors are involved: size of the organizational unit, and process maturity. Small size and high process maturity clearly help.

Common misconceptions (for instance that object orientation or setting up a repository automatically mean successful reuse) lead to the likelihood of overlooking the importance of addressing all the points above. Check the ownership of processes and requirements, especially in the case of embedded real-time software. Changing non-reuse-specific processes and adding reuse-specific processes will be much more difficult when ownership of those processes lies elsewhere, that is when subcontracting is involved.

3. *Reuse implementation*

Each of the points above has to be addressed through further lower-level choices.

- *Change non-reuse-specific processes.* Requirements definition and analysis, high-level design, and testing, all require specific changes to take into account the availability of assets. Project management is impacted too, as far as scheduling, costs and productivity are concerned.

- *Add reuse-specific processes.* Domain analysis might or might not be used to drive the identification of reusable assets. Assets could be smaller or larger in size, including design and requirements or not. They could be developed from scratch, or reengineered from legacy. They could be produced and maintained either by a specific group or by application projects, and, either well before projects need them or just in time for their first use.

- *Address human factors.* One or more techniques (such as training, awareness events, discussion groups, newsletters) can be used. Rewards systems alone are not sufficient.

- *Set up a repository*. A specific tool, add-ons to the configuration management system, or plain configuration management, are all possible options.

The availability of resources in the company, usually related to its size, should be carefully considered in arriving at decisions that can be sustained. Provided the approach is sustainable, integrated, and adapted to the context, any combination of choices is acceptable.

Overall, successful cases always tried to minimize change. They retained their existing development approach and chose reuse technology to fit that approach. They often used their existing configuration management tool for the repository. The advantage here lies in introducing as few changes at a time as possible and in building on existing knowledge, skills and tools. The central question becomes: what is worth changing and what is not? Successful cases teach us that change should focus primarily on processes and roles. Development technology and supporting tools can be changed later, if necessary.

Changes to processes and roles should be affordable. The companies' choices varied considerably; yet, if we relate them to their size and available resources, a logic appears. For instance, only bigger companies can sustain a separate reuse group. The same applies to domain engineering, a process that only few can afford. Finally, assets are developed in advance by the bigger companies, while the others develop assets just in time for the first reuse.

10.4 Conclusion

The survey covered projects in large and small companies, working in a variety of business domains. Most of them produce software with high commonality between applications, have a good-to-reasonable process maturity level, and use an object-oriented or procedural development approach. Despite this apparent potential for success, around one-third of projects failed.

Failures were due to not introducing reuse processes, not modifying non-reuse processes, and not considering human factors. The most important cause was the lack of commitment by top management, or their non-awareness of the importance of the previous factors, often coupled with the technical belief that using the object-oriented approach or setting up a repository would automatically lead to success in reuse.

Given reuse potential due to commonality among applications, the success of a reuse initiative depends on a mix of features.

- Overall, success in a reuse initiative is a technology transfer endeavour, which requires as a sine qua non commitment of management.

- The approach to designing a reuse programme seems to require that a certain minimal standard set of considerations should be properly taken into account. They include initiating reuse-specific processes, modifying non-reuse-specific processes, and addressing human factors.

- If the approach is standard, the way of deploying it is not. Each element listed above must be approached according to the context of the company.

These results are in conformance with other studies already performed. However, this is the first study, to our knowledge, to use interviews, providing a somewhat higher degree of confidence in the results. Further, small companies were also involved, in a variety of countries and cultures.

To advance the state of practice, the results of the study should be used to eradicate the misunderstandings that are still popular among practitioners. Unfortunately, reuse is seldom part of software engineering curricula, so students do not contribute to advancing the state of knowledge when they are hired in companies. It is predictable that there will be a long delay before sensible advances are made.

Finally, a shift may be observed, away from limiting reuse to coding assets, toward reusable components, acquired or developed internally. Consequently, research on reuse should focus more on the implications of the component paradigm on processes, organisations and tools.

References

1. Bayer, J., Flege, O., Knauber, P. *et al.* (1999) PuLSE: A Methodology to Develop Software Product Lines, *Symposium on Software Reusability (SSR99)*, May 1999.
2. Weiss, D.M. and Lai, C.T.R. (1999) *Software Product-Line Engineering: A Family-Based Software Development Approach*, Addison-Wesley.

Acronyms

AFE   Application Family Engineering
The development of a functional architecture for a product line or family of applications (cf CSE).

API   Application Programming Interface
A set of services offered by a library or component to its users. Defines the protocol required to use the asset.

ami   Application of Metrics in Industry
A method for implementing software metrics programmes, based on the GQM method (qv); also the name of the project which developed the method.

API   Application Programming Interface
A set of services offered by a library or component to its users. Defines the protocol required to use the asset.

ASP   Active Server Pages
Microsoft internet client access technology for incorporating executable code (generally Visual Basic), running on a server, into static HTML pages. ASP+ is a new enhanced version.

B2B   Business-to-Business
The use of the internet in the delivery of products and services between businesses.

CASE   Computer Aided Software Engineering
The use of software tools to support the software process.

CCM   CORBA Component Model
Extension of EJB, based on CORBA middleware but targeted to several languages.

CM   Configuration Management
A key software practice involving all aspects of work product management (including identification, definition, change control, status reporting, integrity, storage, release).

CMIP   Common Management Information Protocol
A standard model and protocol for network and systems management.

CMM   Capability Maturity Model
A class of models that can be used to assess the effectiveness of a set of processes in terms of so-called maturity levels. The best known is the CMM for Software, originating from the SEI (qv).

CMS   Configuration Management System
A system to support the tasks of identifying, defining and baselining work products, controlling their modification and release, recording and reporting their status, and controlling their storage, handling and delivery.

COM   Component Object Model
Microsoft framework standard for components running on a single machine. COM+ (also known as DCOM) is an extension for distributed computing.

CORBA   Common Object Request Broker Architecture
OMG middleware framework standard for components distributed across heterogeneous networks.

COTS   Commercial Off-The-Shelf
Refers to commercial assets that are acquired externally.

CRM   Customer Relationship Management

CSE   Component System Engineering
Developing reusable components for use within a product line or family of applications (cf AFE).

DBMS   Data Base Management System

DCOM   Distributed Component Object Model
Microsoft middleware for components distributed across networks of Windows platforms. Provides distribution and transaction management services.

DoD 2167A   Department of Defense: Standard 2167A
A standard for software development in defence applications.

DTD   Document Type Definition
Defines the meaning of XML documents, beyond their syntax, thus facilitating their interpretation.

EJB   Enterprise JavaBeans
Standard for server-side business components implemented in Java, specifying the interfaces between such components and application servers.

ERP   Enterprise Resource Planning
Generally refers to COTS software packages that provide ERP features.

ESPRIT   European Strategic Programme for Research in Information
  Technology
  A major programme of collaborative research and development, part-
  funded by the European Commission, which ran in the 1980s and 1990s.
  ESPRIT projects included ami, REBOOT and SURPRISE (qqv).

FODA   Feature-Oriented Domain Analysis
  A domain engineering method originating from the SEI (qv).

GDMO   Guidelines for Definition of Managed Objects
  A standard for defining objects in a network in a consistent way; part of
  the CMIP standard (qv).

GQM   Goal–Question–Metric
  A method for deriving software metrics from business goals.

GUI   Graphical User Interface

HTML   Hyper-Text Markup Language
  Standard file format for web pages.

HTTP   Hyper-Text Transport Protocol
  Communication protocol used to transfer pages and files from a web
  server to a web browser.

ICE   Information and Content Exchange
  W3C protocol used to exchange data between web sites.

IDL   Interface Definition Language
  Any language used to express component services or interfaces. The best
  known is CORBA IDL, used to define distributed object services.

IIOP   Internet Inter-ORB Protocol
  Standard protocol for communicating within a CORBA platform or
  between two CORBA platforms.

ISO 9001   International Organisation for Standardisation: Standard 9001
  An international standard for quality management systems.

ISO 12207   Application of Metrics in Industry
  An international standard defining software processes.

IT   Information Technology
  This established term is often now replaced by the wider ICT (Information
  and Communication Technology).

J2EE   Java 2 Enterprise Edition
  Standard for Java technologies, including EJB and JSP, led by Sun
  and defined by a consortium of companies. Provides an extensive

environment for developing Internet-based business or middleware frameworks.

JSP Java Server Pages
Technology for incorporating Java code, running on a server, into HTML pages. Useful for accessing back-end systems (in particular EJBs) from a web application.

KLOC Thousands of Lines Of Code
A measure of program size.

LAN Local Area Network

MTS Microsoft Transaction Server
Provides distribution and transaction management services necessary for implementing any business layer.

OLE Object Linking and Embedding
Microsoft environment for component development and execution on a desktop.

OMG Object Management Group
Industrial consortium of over seven hundred organizations in charge of the standardization of object technologies. Its main achievements are CORBA, CCM and UML.

OO Object-Oriented, Object Orientation
Refers to an approach to software development based on the identification and classification of entities in the problem domain and their behaviours.

OOA Object-Oriented Analysis

OOD Object-Oriented Design

OOP Object-Oriented Programming

OOT Object-Oriented Technology
Combines OOA, OOD and OOP.

ORB Object Request Broker
A service enabling objects to exchange requests and responses in a distributed heterogeneous environment. See CORBA, IIOP.

PLP Product Line Practice
The business, organizational and technical practices of handling a group of software products which share a common managed set of features designed to satisfy specific needs of a selected market or mission.

RCR   Relative Cost of Reuse
Cost of reusing an asset or group of assets as a proportion of the estimated cost of developing them from scratch.

RCWR   Relative Cost of Writing for Reuse
Cost of developing an asset or group of assets for reuse as a proportion of the estimated cost of developing for single use only.

REBOOT   Reuse Based on Object-Oriented Techniques
A comprehensive reuse method, noted for introducing the distinction between developing for reuse and developing with reuse; also the name of the project which developed the method.

RL   Reuse Level
Reused software as a proportion of total software produced.

RMI   Remote Method Invocation
Protocol used by Java objects located on different machines to communicate remotely.

ROI   Return On Investment
Net profits attributable to a given investment, expressed as a proportion of that investment. There are a variety of ways in which ROI can be calculated.

SADT   Structured Analysis and Design Technique
A software development method based on a number of structured notations including actigrams and datagrams.

SA/RT   Structured Analysis/Real-Time
A software development method based on a variety of structured notations including data flow diagrams, control flow diagrams and state transition diagrams.

SCADA   Supervision, Control And Data Acquisition
Refers to a category of systems aiming at supervising and controlling industrial processes.

SEI   Software Engineering Institute
An institute of Carnegie Mellon University (Pittsburgh USA), funded by the US Department of Defense, to improve software engineering practice.

SEPG   Software Engineering Process Group
Group responsible for the definition, maintenance and improvement of the software process in an organization.

SME   Small or Medium-Size Enterprise

SNMP   Simple Network Management Protocol
A standard model and protocol for network and systems management.

SPC   Software Productivity Consortium
An organisation based in Virginia USA, that undertakes research and technology transfer projects for the benefit of member organisations. In particular it has produced a Reuse Adoption Guidebook.

SPI   Software Process Improvement
Any actions, or concerted programme, undertaken with the aim of making an organization's software process more effective and increasing its business value.

SURPRISE   Survey on Possibilities of Reuse in Software Engineering
The name of the project which undertook the studies on which this book reports.

SWOT   Strengths, Weaknesses, Opportunities, Threats
A systematic approach to analysing the present situation of an organisation, in terms of both its internal state and its external environment.

TNM   Telecommuncations Network Management
A class of software application systems.

UML   Unified Modelling Language
Standard method-independent language from OMG for specifying, visualizing, constructing and documenting the artefacts of software systems.

UP   Unified Process
Definition of a standard terminology and framework for defining software processes.

W3C   World Wide Web Consortium
Consortium in charge of the standardisation of internet and web technologies (see ICE).

XML   eXtensible Markup Language
A meta-language in which markup languages for different classes of documents can be defined.

Selected Bibliography

The authors recommend the following few titles as an essential first-stage reading list.

I. Jacobson, M. Griss, P. Jonsson (1997) *Software Reuse: Architecture, Process and Organization for Business Success.* Addison-Wesley.

One of the most recent reference books on reuse. The book opens with examples of successful software reuse (Ericsson, AT&T, Motorola, IBM and Microsoft), showing the possibilities of pay-off from reuse. The authors then address the following main aspects of reuse.

- Business and management: what is reuse, what are the basic principles, what are the business needs?

- Processes: they define three engineering processes, based on UML modelling, respectively aimed at developing applications families, components and individual applications.

- Organization: how should reuse be implemented and managed within a company.

This is a complete and detailed book.

E.A. Karlsson (editor) (1995) *Software Reuse: a Holistic Approach.* John Wiley.

This book is based on the results of an ESPRIT project named 'REBOOT'. It defines a complete methodological approach to reuse, based on object oriented development. It defines two main reuse processes – development *for* reuse and development *with* reuse – and gives guidelines for applying these processes with object oriented technology. Some examples in C++ are given. Management activities are also described, including possible organizations, repository management, metrics and reuse introduction.

S. Hallsteinsen, M. Paci (1997) *Experiences in Software Evolution and Reuse : Twelve Real World Projects.* Springer-Verlag.

This book presents real-life case histories. Several examples of large organisations practising reuse are described. They include mainly European banks and industrial companies (telecommunications, manufacturing, aerospace). For each case, the different contexts, approaches and results are presented. A synthesis summarises main data, and presents recurrent business scenarios and lessons learned.

J. Poulin (1996) *Measuring Software Reuse*. Addison Wesley.

This book presents a comprehensive, pragmatic and documented view of methods and tools to measure reuse processes and products. The metrics point of view compels reuse adopters to a more rigorous approach that helps in avoiding or recognising common problems and pitfalls.

Index

W

W3C 149

Wall Street traders 8

white-box customisation (see
    customisation)

white-box reuse 15, 16, 72, 174

workproduct 5, 7, 10, 12, 18, 31, 33, 35, 50,
    55, 59, 85, 114, 117, 121, 123, 124,
    166, 195

work structure 101, 110

PRACTITIONER SERIES

Series Editor: *Ray Paul*
Editorial Board: *Frank Bott, Nic Holt,*
                 Kay Hughes, Elizabeth Hull,
                 Richard Nance, Russel Winder and Sion Wyn

These books are written by practitioners for practitioners.

They offer thoroughly practical hands-on advice on how to tackle specific problems. So, if you are already a practitioner in the development, exploitation or management of IS/IT systems, or you need to acquire an awareness and knowledge of principles and current practice in an IT/IS topic fast then these are the books for you.

All books in this series will be clear, concise and problem solving and will cover a wide range of areas including:
- systems design techniques
- performance modelling
- cost and estimation control
- software maintenance
- quality assurance
- database design and administration
- HCI
- safety critical systems
- distributed computer systems
- internet and web applications
- communications, networks and security
- multimedia, hypermedia and digital libraries
- object technology
- client-server
- formal methods
- design approaches
- IT management

All books are, of course, available from all good booksellers (who can order them even if they are not in stock), but if you have difficulties you can contact the publishers direct, by telephoning +44 (0) 1483 418822 (in the UK & Europe), +1/212/4 60/15 00 (in the USA), or by emailing orders@svl.co.uk

www.springer.de   www.springer-ny.com